C is for COOKING

Recipes from the Street

1807
WILEY
2007

John Wiley & Sons, Inc.

Susan McQuillan
Photographer: Ben Fink

This book is dedicated to Molly, who brought Elmo and the gang into my life and changed it for the better, forever. Special thanks go to our extremely talented panel of young recipe testers and tasters: Molly McQuillan, Danielle Tull, Simone Robbennolt, Sabrina Xuereb, Starr Silver, Sydney Caputo, Tess Brennan, Talia Crawford, and Ruby Serafin. You guys are the best! —SUSAN MCQUILLAN

Contributing Writer and Editor   Leslie A. Kimmelman

Sesame Workshop
Vice President, Publishing,
Home Video, and Audio   Scott Chambers
Editorial Director   Jennifer A. Perry
Senior Curriculum Specialist Jane Park

John Wiley & Sons
Publisher   Natalie Chapman
Senior Editor   Linda Ingroia
Production Director   Diana Cisek
Senior Production Editor   Ava Wilder
Manufacturing Manager   Kevin Watt

Cover and Interior Designer Colleen Pidel
Food Stylist   Joe Tully

Copyright © 2007 by Sesame Workshop
"Sesame Workshop"®, "Sesame Street"®, and associated characters, trademarks, and design elements are owned and licensed by Sesame Workshop. © 2007 Sesame Workshop. All Rights Reserved.

Sesame character photography © 2007 Sesame Workshop

Food photography © 2007 Ben Fink

Wiley Bicentennial Logo Designer   Richard J. Pacifico

Published by John Wiley & Sons, Inc., Hoboken, New Jersey

Published simultaneously in Canada

Library of Congress Cataloging-in-Publication Data
McQuillan, Susan, 1953-
Sesame Street "C" is for Cooking : Recipes from the Street / Susan McQuillan.
   p. cm.
Includes index.
 ISBN   978-0-471-79101-0 (hardcover: alk. paper)
 1. Cookery—Juvenile literature. 2. Sesame Street (Television program) 1. Title.
TX652.5.M357 2007
641.5'123—dc22

                    2006016017

Toppan Leefung Packaging & Printing (Dongguan) Co., Ltd.
Jin Ju Guan Li Qu, Da Ling Shan Town Dongguan, PRC
September 2009

Printed in China
13   12   11

There are twiddlebugs of many colors that look like this in this book. Can you count how many?
Answer: see page 127

contents

Page 44

Page 92

Introduction

The goal of *"C" is for Cooking* is to bring parents and young children together to have fun cooking good food that the entire family can enjoy. Your kitchen is about to become a creative testing ground, a place where children can learn a lot about food, healthy eating habits, and cooking, as well as concepts related to math, literacy, science, and cultural aware- ness—not to mention cleaning up after themselves! True, cooking with young children can take some time and get a little messy. Be ready to have to repeat directions. Be ready for the meals to take longer to prepare than if you did it yourself. Be ready for some mess, too! But most of all, be ready for a whole lot of fun with your children!

> But most of all, be ready for a whole lot of fun with your children!

Cooking, and the learning experience attached to it, actually starts wherever you buy your food. When time allows, bookmark the recipe you plan to prepare with your child, and take this book to the market so you can use the recipe as a shopping list. Let your children help find and choose the ingredients you need. Take advantage of their natural curiosity as you intro- duce them to different types of foods and food colors, textures, flavors, and smells. You can also help your children learn about different methods of storing and preserving food and the wealth of information that's found on food packaging, including ingredients lists, expiration dates, and the nutrition facts labels.

With your guidance, exploring food can help children improve their fine motor skills and eye-hand coordination. Following recipes can reinforce basic math and reading skills and help children begin to learn how to follow sequential directions. By starting early and involving your preschoolers in the kitchen to learn how to prepare foods from scratch, you are building a foundation for them to make smart food choices throughout their lifetime as well as helping them develop a taste for wholesome, homemade food.

But the best part of cooking with children? It happens when you sit down together to eat and see the proud look on your child's face as she shares food that she helped to make. The more time your child spends in the kitchen helping with meal preparation, the more curious and open-minded she'll become about food. In the end, cooking with children is as much about the shared family experience and memories formed as it is about helping kids learn new skills and develop a positive relationship with food.

Note: Once you let your kids in the kitchen, you're going to have a hard time getting them out!

Most children love to cook. They even love the responsibility of cleaning up. Whenever you can, find something for your child to do in the kitchen, something that will keep him busy while you work and make him feel that he's contributing to the meal you're preparing. It will pay off. By the time your child is seven or eight years old, he or she will be a real help to you in the kitchen.

Before you Begin

The recipes in *"C" is for Cooking* were designed for, worked on, and taste-tested by young children and their families. When cooking with kids, it helps to have extra supplies on hand, such as child-friendly measuring cups, measuring spoons, plastic and metal mixing bowls, wooden spoons for stirring, and plastic serrated knives for cutting soft food. If you want your child to wear an apron, buy one that's an appropriate size.

What seems like a small, mindless task to you—say, peeling a banana or cutting a zucchini into coin shapes—is a huge responsibility for a child. But it's a welcome responsibility, because preparing food for others to eat instills a tremendous sense of pride and accomplishment in young children.

Every recipe in this cookbook highlights at least one task that a young child can perform. Choose recipes with steps that you think your own child can accomplish. The age appropriate list of tasks provided on the next page is adapted from The National Network for Child Care's recommendations for cooking with children.

Trust your own instincts—if a task seems too difficult for your child, don't frustrate him by making him do it. Invite him to help in another way.

Remember that even a very young child can help by handing you an ingredient or a small utensil, such as a wooden spoon.

Children of different ages exhibit varying degrees of skill in the kitchen, but for the most part, **an average two-year-old** can help:

- wash and scrub fruits and vegetables;
- wipe off the work surface;
- carry utensils and small equipment to the work surface;
- crush crackers and cookies into crumbs;
- snap the stem end from green beans;
- tear up lettuce and spinach leaves;
- dip one ingredient into another;
- arrange foods on baking sheets and trays;

and **an average three-year-old** can do whatever a two-year-old can do, plus help:

- cut soft foods with a plastic serrated knife;
- pour measured liquid ingredients into a bowl of dry ingredients;
- stir or whisk ingredients together;
- mix batter;

while **an average four- and five-year-old** can do all of the above, plus help:

- measure dry ingredients;
- mash soft foods together;
- peel a banana or an orange if the skin has been loosened for them;
- crack an egg into a bowl (but have some extra eggs on hand!);
- shape meatballs;
- set the table to eat;
- clear the table after eating.

Slightly older siblings and friends can help plan the meal, read the recipe out loud, supervise younger cooks, and take on some of the more complicated cooking tasks, such as peeling hard-cooked eggs, juicing lemons, leveling off dry ingredients, and measuring liquid ingredients.

Remember: Children must be supervised in the kitchen at all times, even when performing age-appropriate tasks.

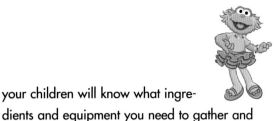

get ReaDY TO get COOKIN'!

In the pages that follow, you'll find more than 50 family-style recipes and ideas written for adults to prepare with children.

kids!

Each recipe contains at least one kids! icon, indicating a step that a child between the ages of two and five could accomplish, depending on the age and skill of the actual child. Also included with the recipes are tips on shortcuts, ingredient substitutions, serving suggestions, and variations. Special features written for the children bring words of culinary wisdom from Elmo and friends, simple math concepts from the Count, culture-related tidbits from Grover, and curiosities from Big Bird and Bert and Ernie. Photographs show how the finished recipes can look. For extra fun at mealtimes, turn to Together Time on page 120.

how TO USE The ReCIPeS In ThIS BOOK

The first step in preparing even the simplest dish is to read the recipe through from beginning to end. That way, you and your children will know what ingredients and equipment you need to gather and prepare a plan for what you're about to do together. Young children can read familiar numbers out loud from the igredient list and pick out favorite letters of the alphabet. Although understanding fractions can be difficult for preschoolers, you can certainly point out "½" in an ingredients list

> Young children can read familiar numbers out loud from the ingredients list and pick out favorite letters of the alphabet.

and explain the concept by showing the amount in a measuring cup or by cutting an apple or a tomato in half and explaining that the two halves make one whole.

All the recipes in this book give a preparation time and cooking time. The preparation time is the average time it will take an adult to prepare the recipe. Depending on the recipe and the circumstances in your own kitchen, this number could be longer. Cooking time is the actual amount of time the food spends on top of the stove or in the oven. The yield, or number of servings, is based on standard serving sizes, not child-size portions. So four servings might actually feed five or six people, depending on individual appetites.

A few other recipe basics to keep in mind for successful cooking:

- Ingredients are listed in the order in which they are used.
- Before you start cooking, measure and prepare all foods as they are written in the ingredients list. If measuring out is inconvenient at that point, make sure the necessary equipment, such as measuring spoons, is conveniently located near the food that will need measuring.
- Turn your oven on at the step indicated so that it's preheated when you're ready to use it.
- A kitchen with children may be a busy and crowded kitchen. To help ensure that everyone has a good time, read Elmo's list of kitchen safety rules out loud with your children before you start cooking (see page 11).

A NOTE ABOUT NUTRITION

The recipes in this book were tested with low-fat (1%) milk and yogurt and, on occasion, with "light" or "part-skim" cheese. This is in keeping with current recommendations from the American Heart Association, the American Academy of Pediatrics, and other health experts, to include low-fat dairy products in the diets of children over the age of two. Low-fat dairy products have the same amount of nutrients as whole dairy products, just less fat. Health experts also recommend using whole grains whenever possible, such as whole grain breads and brown rice, as well as plenty of fresh fruits and vegetables every day. Keep a variety of healthy options around the house to encourage your children to choose foods with low sugar and fat content.

Finally, watch portion sizes. Eating appropriate amounts will make it possible for your family to enjoy all its favorite foods—and try some new ones, too!

A NOTE ABOUT CHILDREN AND CHOKING

Young children's teeth are still developing, which means they are still learning to chew and swallow properly. It's important to slice some foods (such as round, firm pieces of vegetables and fruits) into smaller pieces that are safe for young children to swallow.

> Be sure to check the ingredients list on all food products.

A NOTE ABOUT CHILDREN AND FOOD ALLERGIES

More than two million American children are diagnosed with food allergies.

Food allergies are especially common among young children, so be cautious of the most common foods that cause allergic reactions, including: peanuts, tree nuts (walnuts, pecans, and other nuts), fish, shellfish, eggs, milk, soy, and wheat. If you're cooking with friends, be sure to find out from parents if any children in your kitchen are allergic to any foods.

Allergic reactions to foods may be mild or very severe, depending on how much of the food the child has ingested and how allergic he or she is. Obviously, if you have a child with a food allergy, it is extremely important to avoid using recipes with ingredients that might cause a reaction. Be sure to check the ingredients list on all food products and avoid any product that doesn't clearly list ingredients on the label.

Remember, too, that children under the age of one year should never be given honey.

Bon Appetit! That's French for "Happy Eating!"

Kitchen Safety

Hi, everybody! Elmo is so happy to see you and so excited to be cooking with you. Elmo knows that it's important to keep safe while cooking. Here are the safety rules that Elmo always follows in the kitchen:

1. Grown-ups must supervise all kitchen activities, including cooking and cleaning up. Make sure there's a grown-up nearby whenever you're working in the kitchen. Always ask that grown-up when you need help preparing food, or if you can't reach something you need.

2. Grown-ups should set aside a special place for you to work in the kitchen. This space should be away from hot things such as stoves, pots, and pans, and away from knives and other sharp objects.

3. If you have long hair, tie it back. And if you have long sleeves, roll them up!

4. Always wash your hands with soap and water before you touch food. You should also wash your hands after you handle raw meat, chicken, turkey, or fish, before you touch anything else. Don't put your fingers in your mouth after you touch food; remember to wash them first! Also, if you have to sneeze or cough into your hands, wash them before you go back to work.

5. Never touch kitchen knives, food processor blades, blender blades, scissors, or any other sharp object. Leave the sharp stuff to the grown-ups! Instead, use a serrated plastic knife to cut soft foods such as zucchini squash, bananas, and canned fruit. But even with a plastic knife, you must be very careful. A grown-up will show you how to cut away from your fingers so you don't get hurt.

6. Never go near a hot stove without a grown-up. Grown-ups are responsible for putting food in the oven, taking it out, and cooking food on top of the stove.

7. Start with a clean kitchen! Help the grown-up wipe off the counter and put away anything you don't need so that you have lots of room to work.

8. Have a grown-up read the recipe out loud before you start cooking. Help the grown-up gather all the food and equipment you need. Whenever you're done with an ingredient, put any leftovers away. The same rule applies to equipment—when you're done with it, put it aside to be cleaned. That way you can keep your work surface organized and safe!

9. Help make the kitchen safe. Remind the grown-up to make sure there are no pot handles sticking out from the stove, that there are no wires hanging off the counter, and that there are no knives or other sharp utensils lying around.

10. Work slowly and carefully, and do just one job at a time.

11. When you sit down to eat, enjoy each bite of your food. Explore all the different flavors and textures. Eat slowly and chew your food well before you swallow.

What do lemons do when they get in trouble?
Elmo knows, Elmo knows! They call for lemon-aid!

sweet SIPS

Even picky eaters love sipping (or slurping!) drinks like refreshing lemonade or smooth and creamy shakes. There's a real health benefit to making your own drinks, too. You can control the amount of sugar they

contain, preserve the natural vitamins in fruit, and add essential minerals like calcium by including yogurt, milk, and—once in a while—ice cream. Making drinks with your kids is also a

simple way to get them "cooking." The drinks here are scrumptious, special treats to try.

BIg BIrD'S SunnY DAYS Lemonade

Preparation time: 10 minutes plus cooling time • Cooking time: 5 minutes

Makes 2½ cups syrup (10 cups lemonade)

This recipe makes condensed lemonade syrup that can be diluted with water to make regular lemonade or with seltzer to make sparkling lemonade. Use the lesser amount of sugar to make a slightly tart lemonade, the higher amount for a sweeter sip.

IngreDIenTS

- 2 cups water
- ¾ to 1 cup sugar
- Juice of 4 large lemons (1 cup)

equIPmenT

- Measuring cups
- Medium saucepan
- Spoon
- Knife
- Juicer
- Storage container with lid (3-cup)
- Drinking glasses

1 Combine the water and sugar in a medium saucepan. Bring to a boil over high heat, stirring to dissolve the sugar.

 2 kids! Roll the lemon on the counter with the palms of your hands, pressing down hard with one hand on top of the other.

3 Halve and juice the lemons. Remove the sugar syrup from the heat and stir in the lemon juice. Set aside to cool completely. You can store the lemonade syrup in a covered container in the refrigerator for up to one week.

 4 kids! To make lemonade, place ¼ cup of lemonade syrup in a glass, add ice cubes, if you like, and fill with water or seltzer.

Lemons are sour. Sugar is sweet. Together they make a real tasty treat!

Big Bird asked his Granny Bird, "Why does rolling a lemon make it juicier?" Granny Bird told him that the juice in a lemon (or orange) is held in sections. When you roll the lemon on the counter and press hard with the palm of your hand before you squeeze it, you crush those sections. That makes it easier for the juice to escape.

TIP:
To make pink lemonade, add a splash of cranberry juice to the mix. To make lemon limeade, use 2 lemons and 6 limes in place of the 4 lemons called for in the recipe.

ROSITA'S strawberry-mango smoothie

Preparation time: 15 minutes • Makes 4 to 6 servings (4 cups)

Fruits are naturally sweet, eaten whole or in a recipe. A pinch of dried mint "wakes up" the flavor of any fruit smoothie, but it's not an essential ingredient in this recipe.

> Mangos grow on trees in warm weather places. I'd do a tango for a mango!

INGREDIENTS

- 2 cups strawberries, green leaves and stems removed
- 1 ripe mango, cut into cubes (about 1 cup)
- 1½ cups low-fat milk
- 1 cup (8 ounces) low-fat vanilla yogurt
- ¼ teaspoon dried mint (optional)
- Ice cubes

EQUIPMENT

- Measuring cups
- Blender
- Drinking glasses

1 Combine the strawberries, mango cubes, and milk in the container of a blender. (Make sure to keep your children's fingers away from the sharp blender blades.) Whirl on high until smooth, about 1 minute.

2 **kids!** Add the yogurt and mint, if using, to the blender.

3 Whirl on high 20 seconds longer.

4 **kids!** Fill drinking glasses with ice cubes.

5 Pour the smoothie over the ice. Serve cold.

TIP:
When you can't find good fresh fruit, substitute equal amounts of partially thawed, frozen mango cubes and whole strawberries.

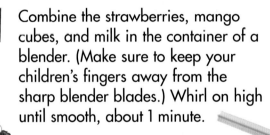

Best Buddies orange crème shake

Preparation time: 5 minutes • Makes 4 servings (4 cups)

This creamy shake tastes just like an orange fruit pop. Yum!

My favorite color—and it matches your nose!

Ingredients
- 2 cups orange juice
- 1 cup (8 ounces) low-fat vanilla yogurt
- 1 cup (2 scoops) low-fat vanilla frozen yogurt or ice cream, softened
- 8 ice cubes

Equipment
- Measuring cups
- 8-cup glass measuring cup or pitcher
- Long-handled wooden spoon
- Four 8-ounce glasses

1 Combine the orange juice, yogurt, and ice cream in an 8-cup glass measuring cup or pitcher.

2 kids! Use a long-handled wooden spoon to stir the orange juice mixture until the ice cream melts.

3 kids! Put two ice cubes in each of four glasses.

4 Divide the shake mixture evenly among the four glasses.

TIP:
To make a semi-frozen, "slushie" drink, crack the ice and use a blender instead of mixing the shake by hand.

"Greetings! I, **Count von Count**, need you to help me count the ice cubes in this recipe. But watch out. Counting ice cubes can be a chilly experience! 1, 2, 3, 4, 5, 6, 7, 8. That's 8 ice cubes, *ah, ah, ah!*"

OScar's Spicy Cider

Preparation time: 10 minutes • Cooking time: 15 minutes • Makes 16 servings (½ cup each)

Everyone knows that worms love apples. So Oscar often makes this drink for his favorite worm pal, Slimey. The mildly spicy, citrus-scented apple cider can be served either warm or cold. It's easy to make, even for grouches!

INGReDIeNTS

- 8 whole cloves
- 4 lemon slices, seeded and halved
- 4 cinnamon sticks
- 4 orange slices, seeded and quartered
- ½ gallon apple cider

eQUIPMENT

- Large saucepan
- Slotted spoon
- Mugs

1 kids! Stick a clove into the white part of each lemon slice. Break each cinnamon stick in half.

2 kids! In a large saucepan, combine the clove-studded lemon slices, cinnamon sticks, and orange slices. Pour in the apple cider with help from a grown-up.

3 Heat just to a boil over medium-high heat. Reduce heat to low and simmer for 10 minutes. Set aside to cool slightly.

4 With a slotted spoon, remove the cinnamon sticks and fruit slices. Ladle into mugs to serve warm, or refrigerate and serve chilled.

TIP:
If you don't have cinnamon sticks, use 1 teaspoon ground cinnamon.

I ♥ trash!

Oscar didn't know what cinnamon was, so he looked it up on the Grouch-wide Web. He found out that cinnamon is a sweet spice made from the bark of a tree. The cinnamon stick is actually the bark, rolled up! Cinnamon bark can also be ground up to make cinnamon powder.

Elmo likes cold milk, too. Elmo drinks it every day!

mommy-and-elmo
hot cocoa float

Preparation time: 2 minutes • Cooking time: 5 minutes • Makes 4 servings (6 ounces each)

This hot cocoa is enriched with real milk chocolate and a scoop of ice-cream topping, so a little goes a long way to satisfy a sweet tooth. Save this dessert-like drink for special occasions, but hot chocolate without topping is tasty and comforting anytime.

ingredients

- ¼ cup sugar
- 2 tablespoons unsweet-ened cocoa powder
- Pinch salt
- 3 cups low-fat milk
- 1 ounce milk chocolate or dark chocolate, cut up
- 4 small scoops low-fat vanilla frozen yogurt or ice cream

equipment

- Measuring cups
- Measuring spoons
- Whisk
- Medium saucepan
- Ice-cream scoop
- Mugs

1 **kids!** Use a whisk to mix together the sugar, cocoa powder, and salt in a medium saucepan. Then slowly whisk in the milk.

2 Bring the milk mixture to a gentle simmer over medium heat, whisking often. Add the chocolate; whisk until blended.

3 **kids!** Put a scoop of the frozen yogurt or ice cream in each mug.

4 Pour the hot cocoa over the ice cream in the mugs.

Do you know why ice cream floats on top of the hot chocolate in your mug? **Elmo** knows! Elmo's mommy told him. It's the same reason Rubber Duckie floats on top of the water in Ernie's bathtub. The ice cream is lighter than the hot chocolate, so the hot chocolate holds it up.

TIP:
To flavor your hot cocoa, substitute different types of ice creams, such as mint chocolate chip or dulce de leche, for the vanilla that's called for in this recipe.

Don't forget to have some delicious oatmeal to start the day! I put jam stripes in mine to match my shirt.

BEST BREAKFASTS

A good breakfast gives your children the energy they need to start the day. A healthy meal in the morning even helps them concentrate and do their best in  school. You know that your children like certain foods, such as pancakes and eggs. But why not have some simple fun "building" a house out of waffles or shaping pancakes into letters and numbers? In this chapter, you'll find ideas like these as well as recipes for all occasions: simple everyday  breakfasts, dishes that can be prepared the night before, and recipes that are great for weekends and mornings when you have more time to cook with your children.

Big Bird's Banana and Berry Delicious Toast

Preparation time: 10 minutes • Cooking time: about 1 minute toasting time

Makes 4 servings (4 slices)

Use this fruity spread in place of butter or plain cream cheese on bread, toast, or bagels.

Ingredients

- 1 ripe banana
- 2 tablespoons light cream cheese
- 1 cup sliced strawberries or kiwis
- 4 slices bread

Equipment

- Small bowl
- Measuring spoons
- Measuring cup
- Fork for mashing
- Toaster
- Knife for spreading

 1 kids! In a small bowl, mash together the banana, the cream cheese, and ¼ cup of the sliced strawberries.

2 Toast the bread.

 3 kids! Spread the banana mixture evenly on the toast slices. Arrange the remaining strawberry slices on top of the banana spread. Enjoy!

> Bread, berries, and bananas all start with the letter B. Think of some other foods that start with the letter B!

TIP:
For a very colorful presentation, use both strawberry and kiwi slices in alternating rows.

Elmo's mommy told **Elmo** why bananas turn brown when they're mashed. Air mixes with the mashed banana and turns the food brown. Scientists call that *oxidation*. Can you say ox–a–day–shun? Wow! You are smart!

COOKIE MONSTER'S
YUMMY PANCAKES WITH STRAWBERRY SAUCE

Preparation time: 10 minutes • Cooking time: about 15 minutes
Makes 4 to 6 servings (about 12 medium-size pancakes)

Macerated berries (that is, sliced berries sprinkled with a little sugar to draw out some of their juice) take the place of syrup as a flavorful but healthier topping.

INGREDIENTS

- 1 pint strawberries, green leaves and stems removed
- 2 tablespoons sugar
- 1½ cups all-purpose flour
- ½ cup whole-wheat flour
- ¼ cup sugar
- 1 tablespoon baking powder
- ½ teaspoon baking soda
- 1 teaspoon salt
- 1 egg
- 1 cup low-fat milk
- 1 cup (8 ounces) low-fat plain yogurt
- 2 tablespoons vegetable oil

EQUIPMENT

- Plastic knife
- Medium bowls (2)
- Measuring cups
- Measuring spoons
- Large bowl
- Forks for stirring and beating
- Nonstick griddle or skillet
- Wide spatula

1 kids! With a plastic knife, slice the strawberries. In a medium bowl, stir together the strawberry slices and the 2 tablespoons sugar. Set aside while making pancakes.

2 In a large bowl, stir together the all-purpose flour, whole-wheat flour, sugar, baking powder, baking soda, and salt until well-mixed.

3 kids! Crack the egg into a medium bowl. (If any pieces of eggshell fall into the bowl, take them out with your fingers before you start stirring. Wash your hands after you've picked out all the pieces of shell.) Then use a fork to stir together the egg, milk, yogurt, and vegetable oil until smooth. Stir the egg mixture into the flour mixture until blended.

4 Lightly grease a nonstick griddle or large skillet and place over medium heat.

Sometimes me make number or letter pancakes. Me can make C pancake, for Cookie Monster.

5 Use a ¼ cup measure to pour the batter onto the skillet, pouring pancakes several inches apart. Cook on one side until small bubbles appear on the top, the pancake starts to puff, and the cooked side is lightly browned, about 1 to 2 minutes. With a wide spatula, carefully turn pancakes. Cook until the other side is lightly browned, about 1 minute longer.

6 Serve the pancakes topped with strawberries and the juice that forms in their bowl.

eImo's
DutCh BaBy PancaKe
WIth Buttery APPLes

Preparation time: 10 minutes • Cooking/Baking time: 18 minutes • Makes 4 servings

A puffy pancake baking in a cake pan and topped with sautéed fruit looks like dessert, but is really a wholesome breakfast food.

InGReDIents

- 2 eggs
- 1 teaspoon vegetable oil
- ½ cup low-fat milk
- ½ cup all-purpose flour
- 2 tablespoons sugar
- ¼ teaspoon salt
- ¼ teaspoon cinnamon
- 1 tablespoon butter
- 2 large apples, peeled and sliced
- Confectioner's sugar for dusting (optional)

eQuIPMent

- Cake pan or baking dish (9-inch)
- Medium bowl
- Fork
- Measuring cups
- Measuring spoons
- Large skillet
- Large spoon
- Wire-mesh sieve

1 Preheat the oven to 425°F. Grease a 9-inch nonstick cake pan, shallow baking dish, or skillet with an ovenproof handle.

2 kids! Crack the eggs into a medium bowl. (If any pieces of eggshell fall into the bowl, take them out with your fingers before you start stirring. Wash your hands after you've picked out all the pieces of shell.) Then use a fork to beat together the eggs, oil, and milk until smooth. Stir until well-blended.

3 Add the flour, sugar, salt, and cinnamon to the bowl. Stir until a smooth batter forms. (A few small lumps are okay.) Pour the batter into the greased dish.

4 Bake the pancake for 10 minutes. Reduce the heat to 350°F. Bake until the pancake is very puffy and lightly browned all over, about 5 to 8 minutes longer.

5 Meanwhile, heat the butter in a large skillet. Add the apples and sauté, stirring often, until the apples are tender and lightly browned, about 10 minutes.

6 To serve, spoon the apples over the pancake.

7 kids! Use a wire-mesh sieve or other fine-mesh strainer to dust the pancake with confectioner's sugar.

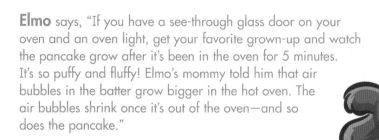

Elmo says, "If you have a see-through glass door on your oven and an oven light, get your favorite grown-up and watch the pancake grow after it's been in the oven for 5 minutes. It's so puffy and fluffy! Elmo's mommy told him that air bubbles in the batter grow bigger in the hot oven. The air bubbles shrink once it's out of the oven—and so does the pancake."

zoe's easy cheesy waffles

Preparation time: 10 minutes • Cooking time: 30 minutes • Makes: 12 (4-inch) waffles

For a change of pace from sweet breakfasts, try these savory waffles with crisp turkey bacon or grilled ham. The sautéed apples that go with the Dutch Baby Pancake (page 28) also make a great topping for these waffles.

ingredients

- 2 eggs
- 1 cup low-fat milk
- 1 cup low-fat plain yogurt
- 1 tablespoon vegetable oil
- 2 cups all-purpose flour
- 2 teaspoons baking powder
- 1 teaspoon baking soda
- ¼ teaspoon salt
- 1½ cups shredded Cheddar, Swiss, or Jack cheese (6 ounces)

equipment

- Waffle iron
- Measuring cups
- Measuirng spoons
- Medium bowls (2)
- Fork for stirring batter
- Cheese grater
- Metal spatula or spoon

1 Preheat the waffle iron.

2 kids! In a medium bowl, beat together the eggs, milk, yogurt, and oil.

3 In a medium bowl, stir together the flour, baking powder, baking soda, and salt until well mixed. Stir in the egg mixture just until evenly moistened.

4 kids! Stir the cheese into the batter just until it's mixed in.

5 Pour enough batter over the hot iron to cover about two-thirds of the grid. With the spatula or spoon, spread the batter to the edges of the grid. Bake the waffles until crisp and brown, about 5 minutes.

• If you don't have a waffle iron, stir another ¼ cup milk into the batter and use it to make pancakes.
• Pancake and waffle batters can be made the night before, covered, and refrigerated until the next day. Just stir the batter and proceed with the recipe in the morning!
• For fun, cut the waffles into shapes, or even "build" a house!

Waffles can be round or rectangle-shaped. The Pilgrims brought waffle recipes with them when they first came to America!

ernie's JeLLY omeLet

Preparation time: 2 minutes • Cooking time: 2 minutes • Makes 2 to 4 servings

This may be a new idea for you, but sweet omelets have been around for more than a hundred years. Recipes can be found in many historical cookbooks. In place of jelly, you might try cut-up fresh fruit or a couple of spoonfuls of applesauce.

Make sure you follow the directions EGGS-actly! Hee, hee, hee!

InGReDIenTS

- 4 eggs
- 1 tablespoon water or low-fat milk
- 2 teaspoons olive or canola oil
- 2 tablespoons strawberry jelly or seedless raspberry jam

equIPmenT

- Small bowls (2)
- Measuring spoons
- Fork
- Medium nonstick skillet with cover
- Nonstick spatula
- Knife

1 kids! Crack the eggs into a small bowl. (If any pieces of egg-shell fall into the bowl, take them out with your fingers before you start stirring them together. Wash your hands after you've picked out all the pieces of shell.) Then use a fork to stir the water or milk into the eggs. Keep stirring until the eggs are completely yellow.

2 Heat the oil in a medium nonstick skillet over medium heat. Add the egg mixture. As the egg sets, lift sections of the omelet with a spatula and tilt the skillet slightly to allow the uncooked egg to run under the cooked egg.

Cover and cook for 30 seconds or until the eggs are just set.

3 kids! While the eggs are cooking, measure the jelly and put it in a small bowl. Stir it well.

4 Pour the jelly over the center of the omelet. With a spatula or fork, lift the omelet and fold it in half. Tilt the skillet to turn the omelet out onto a plate. Cut into wedges and serve.

TIP: Although grape is a favorite jelly flavor with kids, it tends to turn gray in the skillet and that makes the omelet seem less appetizing. It's probably best to stick to bright red-, orange-, or yellow-colored jelly fillings.

"It is I, **Count von Count**, with today's number of the day. Is it 1? Is it 2? Is it 3? Is it 4? It's 4! Today's number is 4! Count out the 4 eggs in the recipe."

ernie's breakfast banana split

Preparation time: 20 minutes • Makes 4 servings

Melon scoops look like ice cream and make this a fun morning meal. Use any combination of your favorite fruits and any crisp cereal your family enjoys in this naturally sweet breakfast treat.

ingredients

- 1 cantaloupe or honeydew melon, halved and seeded
- ½ cup fresh pineapple or kiwi cubes
- ½ cup blueberries
- ¼ cup low-fat lemon yogurt
- 2 bananas
- 2 tablespoons honey (optional)
- 1 cup crispy cold cereal, such as granola

equipment

- Small ice-cream scoop
- Plate or baking sheet
- Measuring cups
- Small bowl for mixing fruit
- Spoon
- Plastic knfie for slicing fruit
- Small serving bowls
- Spoon or honey dipper for drizzing honey

1 Use a small ice-cream scoop to scoop out rounds of melon. Place the melon scoops on a plate or baking sheet and store in the freezer while you prepare the banana and toppings.

2 kids! In a small bowl, toss together the pineapple cubes and the blueberries. Stir in the yogurt. Set aside.

3 kids! Use a plastic knife to cut the bananas in half, crosswise. Cut each half in half again, lengthwise. Place 2 banana pieces in the bottom of 4 small bowls. Top with the scoops of melon from the freezer.

4 kids! Spoon the pineapple mixture over the melon. Drizzle evenly with honey, if using. Sprinkle evenly with cereal.

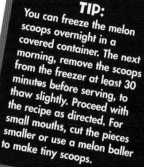

TIP:
You can freeze the melon scoops overnight in a covered container. The next morning, remove the scoops from the freezer at least 30 minutes before serving, to thaw slightly. Proceed with the recipe as directed. For small mouths, cut the pieces smaller or use a melon baller to make tiny scoops.

It is I, Grover, your furry adorable monster globe-trotter, back from a trip to the island of Hawaii, where pineapples grow. *Halakahiki* means "pineapple" in Hawaiian. Say ha-la-ka-hee-kee. Very good! You can speak Hawaiian!

grover's egg and sausage strata

Preparation time: 15 minutes plus sitting time. Resting time: 4 hours or overnight •
Cooking/Baking time: 50 minutes • Makes 6 servings

A strata is a casserole—and a breakfast strata is one that you assemble the night before serving. The next morning you can just pop it in the oven for a fuss-free breakfast or brunch dish. This recipe is simple and versatile. It's perfect for company—or for those times when you're anticipating a busy morning.

ingredients

- 1 teaspoon vegetable oil
- 8 ounces sweet turkey sausage or other type of sausage, casings removed
- 6 slices bread
- 1½ cups shredded Cheddar, Colby, or Monterey Jack cheese
- 6 eggs
- 2 cups low-fat milk
- 1 tablespoon spicy brown or Dijon-style mustard

equipment

- Baking dish (11 x 7 inches)
- Large nonstick skillet
- Nonstick spatula
- Measuring cups
- Large bowl
- Measuring spoons
- Fork for stirring
- Toothpicks
- Plastic wrap

1 Lightly grease an 11 x 7–inch baking dish.

2 Heat the oil in a large nonstick skillet. Add the sausage, stirring often, until the meat is browned and cooked through, about 5 minutes.

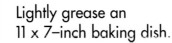

3 kids! Line the baking dish with overlapping slices of bread.

4 Spoon the sausage on top of the bread. Sprinkle evenly with the cheese.

5 kids! Crack the eggs into a large bowl. (If any pieces of eggshell fall into the bowl, take them out with your fingers before you start stirring them together. Wash your hands after you've picked out all the pieces of shell.) Then use a fork to stir together the eggs, milk, and mustard until smooth. Pour over the bread mixture. Cover and refrigerate for at least 4 hours or overnight.

The next time you crash land and smash lots of eggs, do not worry. Just use those cute broken eggs to make this recipe.

6 To bake, preheat the oven to 350°F. Bake the strata, uncovered, until the top is puffed and browned and a toothpick inserted in the center comes out clean, about 45 minutes. Remove the dish from the oven and let stand for 15 minutes before serving.

TIP:
Personalize this strata: Substitute an equal amount of cubed ham, crumbled bacon, sliced chicken-apple sausage, or ordinary pork breakfast sausage for the turkey sausage used in this recipe. Use any type of bread your family prefers. Cut some fat by using reduced-fat and low-fat cheeses and milk. Add leftover vegetables, such as cooked tomatoes, zucchini, or sweet peppers.

Abby Cadabby's
PUMPKIN MUFFINS

Preparation time: 10 minutes • Baking time: 25 minutes • Makes 12 servings (12 muffins)

Unlike most muffins, which are best the day they're baked, the pumpkin and yogurt in these muffins help keep them moist and tender for several days.

INGREDIENTS

- 1½ cups all-purpose flour
- 2 teaspoons baking powder
- ½ teaspoon baking soda
- ½ teaspoon cinnamon
- ¼ teaspoon salt
- ¼ teaspoon ground ginger
- 1 egg
- ⅔ cup packed light brown sugar
- ¼ cup vegetable oil
- ½ cup canned pumpkin
- ½ cup low-fat plain yogurt
- 1 cup uncooked oatmeal (old-fashioned or quick cooking)
- ½ cup golden or dark seedless raisins (optional)

EQUIPMENT

- Muffin pan (for 12 cups)
- Measuring cups
- Measuring spoons
- Small bowls (2)
- Large bowl
- Fork for stirring
- Toothpicks
- Cooling rack

1 Preheat the oven to 350°F. Grease 12 muffin cups.

2 In a small bowl, stir together the flour, baking powder, baking soda, cinnamon, salt, and ginger. Set aside.

3 kids! Crack the egg into a small bowl. (If any pieces of eggshell fall into the bowl, take them out with your fingers before you start stirring.

Wash your hands after you've picked out all the pieces of shell.) Then, in a large bowl, use a fork to stir together the sugar and oil until blended. Stir in the egg, pumpkin, and yogurt until blended.

4 Stir in the flour mixture just until blended.

Abby says, "Pumpkins grow along the ground on vines—not on trees, like apples. And pumpkins, like other orange fruits and vegetables, make your eyes and heart stronger. I just wish they made my wings grow faster!"

5 kids! Gently stir in the oatmeal and the raisins, if using, just until incorporated.

6 kids! Use a ¼ cup measure to scoop the batter into the muffin cups. (Check to be sure each muffin cup is filled about two-thirds of the way full.)

7 Bake the muffins until a toothpick inserted in the center comes out clean, about 25 minutes. Turn the muffins out onto a rack to cool slightly. Serve the muffins warm or at room temperature. Store in a covered container for up to 3 days.

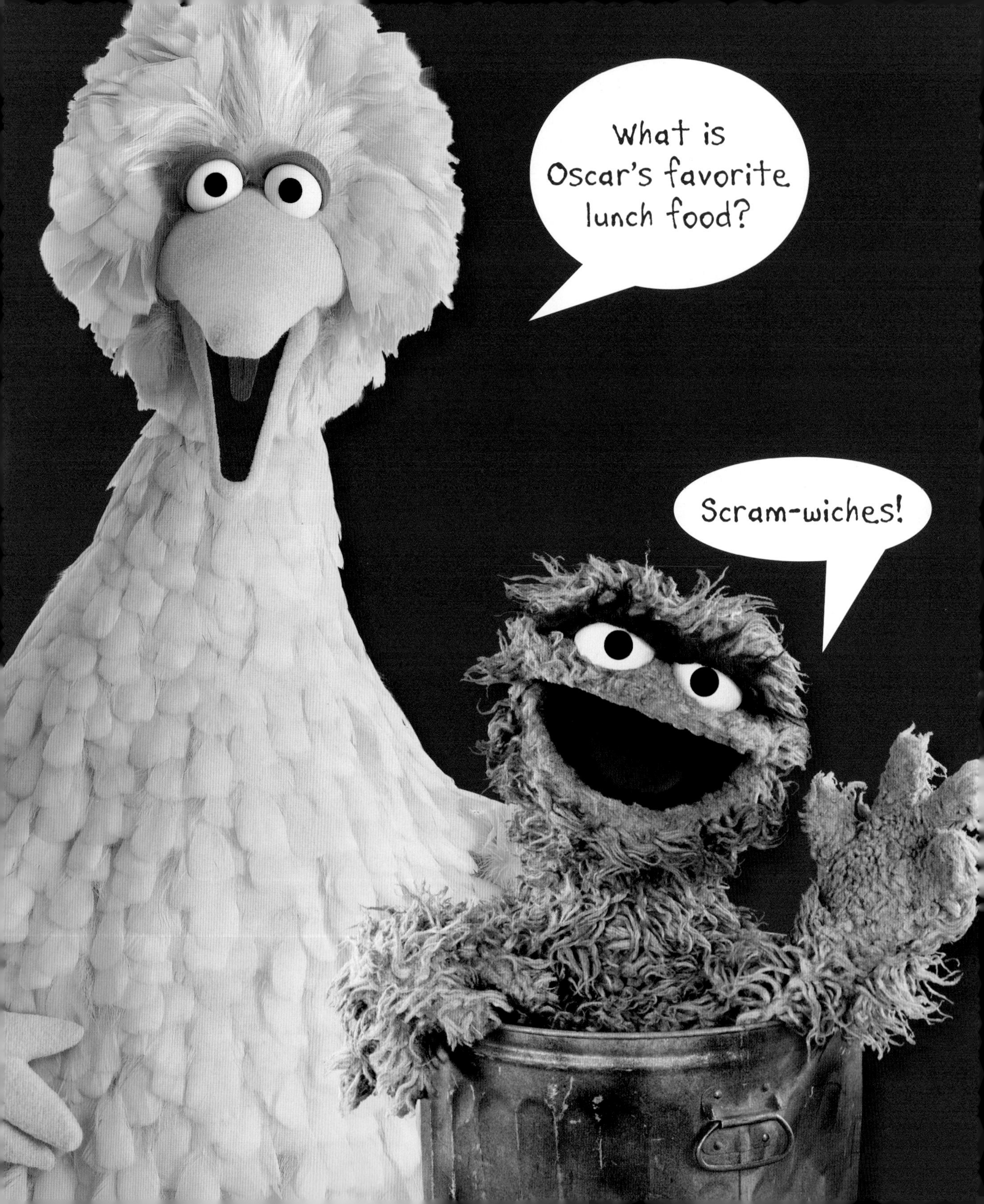
What is Oscar's favorite lunch food?
Scram-wiches!

Lunches to munch on

Whether your children  eat their midday meal at home or at school, lunch is sure to be more enthusiastically received (and eaten!) if they have a hand in making it themselves. Many favorites that  are cooked and served warm at home, such as chicken nuggets and quesadillas, can also be packed for travel and enjoyed cold or at room temperature.

Dum-de-dum. Yum-de-yum.

cookie monster's
homemade peanut Butter sandwiches

Preparation time: 5 minutes • Makes 1¼ cups

There are several good reasons to make your own peanut butter. From a nutritional standpoint, you can control the oil, sugar, and salt content. It's also a great opportunity for children to see exactly how one of their favorite processed foods is actually made.

INGREDIENTS
- 1 pound (3 cups) dry-roasted peanuts (unsalted or lightly salted)
- 1 to 2 tablespoons olive oil

EQUIPMENT
- Measuring cups
- Measuring spoons
- Large bowl
- Large stirring spoon
- Food processor
- Rubber spatula
- Storage container with lid (2-cup)

1 In a large bowl, combine the peanuts and the oil. With a spoon, stir to mix well.

2 Pour the oiled peanuts into a food processor. Process until very smooth, 3 to 4 minutes.

3 Using a rubber spatula, transfer the peanut butter to a container with a tight-fitting lid. Store in the refrigerator for up to two weeks.

Cookie Monster says, "Me know that peanuts make muscles and bones strong. Me also know that homemade peanut butter and banana sandwiches very delicious."

TIP:
This recipe makes a relatively smooth peanut butter. To make chunky peanut butter, set aside ½ cup of peanuts and proceed with the recipe. Once you have a smooth, creamy butter, add the reserved peanuts to the food processor and process for 15 to 20 seconds. If you like, you can add a pinch of salt or a tablespoon or two of honey.

peanut butter sandwich ideas

- Peanut butter on whole grain toast with crisp turkey bacon bits
- Peanut butter with sliced bananas and honey on toasted English muffin
- Peanut butter with grated carrot on cinnamon raisin bread
- Peanut butter with grated apple or pear on cinnamon raisin bread

- Stack 'em sandwich: Spread 2 slices of bread with peanut butter, another 2 slices with jam; stack the slices, alternating peanut butter and jelly. Cut into fourths to make 4 tall stacked sandwiches.
- Sandwich cut-outs: Turn everyday PB&J sandwiches into special treats using cookie cutters in assorted shapes and sizes. Use theme cookie cutters (Halloween pumpkins; Thanksgiving turkeys; Christmas trees) for holidays and special events.

Big Bird's egghead salad

Preparation time: 10 minutes • Makes 4 servings

Making faces on food is creative fun. It may help children respond positively to foods they've never tried or don't normally eat. Make a sample egghead for your children to use as inspiration, then let them create their own faces.

INGREDIENTS

- 2 hard-cooked eggs
- 4 green or black olives, sliced
- 4 corn kernels
- 4 slivers of sweet red pepper
- 2 carrots, shredded
- Shredded lettuce leaves
- Salad dressing

EQUIPMENT

- Knife
- Salad plates (4)
- Assorted small bowls
- Grater

1 Halve the eggs lengthwise and place each half, cut-side-down, on a salad plate. Sort the remaining ingredients into individual bowls.

2 kids! Make faces on the egg halves using olive slices for eyes, a corn kernel for the nose, a sliver of red pepper for the mouth, and shredded carrot for the hair. Surround the egg with shredded lettuce leaves. Use other vegetables—and your imagination—to make more faces.

3 Serve the salad with dressing on the side for pouring or dipping.

TIP: Follow the suggestions to create a face, but use any other foods you think will work. For instance, instead of an egg, try a trimmed boiled potato for the face.

ROSita's
Pita Pizzas

Preparation time: 10 minutes • Baking time: 15 minutes • Makes 4 servings (4 pockets)

The same ingredients (and flavor) of a regular pizza are packed into a pita pocket!

Say "Rosita" and "pita." They rhyme!

1 Preheat the oven to 375°F.

2 kids! In a medium bowl, combine the shredded cheese, tomato sauce, and oregano.

3 Place 2 tomato slices in each pita pocket, if desired. Fill each pocket with ¼ cup cheese mixture. Wrap pita pockets individually in foil and seal the packets.

TIP:
For Tex-Mex pita pizzas, add ½ teaspoon chili powder to the cheese mix.

4 Bake the pita pockets until the filling is heated through, 12 to 15 minutes. Remove the packets from the oven and let the packets cool for several minutes before opening.

INGREDIENTS
- Two 6-inch whole-wheat or other pita rounds, halved
- 1 cup shredded part-skim mozzarella cheese
- ½ cup tomato sauce
- ¼ teaspoon dried oregano
- 8 thin slices tomato (optional)

EQUIPMENT
- Cheese grater
- Measuring cups
- Measuring spoons
- Medium bowl
- Aluminum foil

The Count says, "I love shapes! What shape is your pita bread before you cut it? What shape are the tomato slices? What else can you find in the kitchen that is the same shape?"

zoe's bowtie salad with tuna & veggies

Preparation time: 10 minutes • Cooking time: 12 minutes

Makes 6 to 8 servings (about 10 cups)

This recipe calls for green beans and cherry tomatoes, but you can add any vegetables your family likes to eat. Some other suggestions: cut-up broccoli, snow peas, asparagus, sweet red pepper.

ingredients

- 12 ounces stubby shaped pasta, such as rotelle, radiatore, elbows, fiori (flowers), small egg bows, or penne
- 8 ounces green beans, trimmed and cut into 1- or 2-inch lengths
- ¼ cup olive oil
- ¼ cup lemon juice
- 2 tablespoons mayonnaise
- Pinch each, salt and pepper
- ½ pint cherry tomatoes, halved (about 12 tomatoes)
- 2 cans (3½ ounces each) tuna packed in water, drained

equipment

- Large saucepan
- Measuring cups
- Measuring spoons
- Large bowl
- Whisk
- Colander or strainer
- Can opener
- Large spoon

1 In a large saucepan of lightly salted boiling water, cook the pasta according to package directions until tender, about 8 to 12 minutes, depending on the type and shape of pasta you use. Add the green beans for the last 4 minutes of cooking time.

2 kids! Meanwhile, in a large bowl, whisk together the olive oil and lemon juice. Whisk in the mayonnaise and a pinch each of salt and pepper. Set aside.

3 Drain the pasta and green beans and add to the bowl with the lemon dressing. Toss until just coated. Add the tomatoes and the tuna. Toss gently, just to combine. Serve at room temperature.

The Count says, "Count the tomatoes before they are cut. How many are there? Count them again after they're cut in half. How many are there now?"

Look! The noodles are the same shape as my barrettes!

TIP:
This is an easy salad to pack for a lunch-to-go. Just remember to put a freezer pack in your child's lunch box.

Bert's Tutti-Frutti Turkey Salad

Preparation time: 15 minutes • Makes 4 servings

If you do most of the preparation, the kids can do most of the mixing. They'll feel that they've made the salad pretty much by themselves.

1 kids! Combine the mayonnaise, yogurt, marmalade, curry powder, and lemon juice in a large bowl. Stir until well-blended.

2 kids! Add the turkey, apples, celery, and scallion. Stir until well-mixed.

3 Serve the salad over lettuce leaves, if you like.

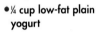

Ingredients

- ½ cup low-fat or other mayonnaise
- ¼ cup low-fat plain yogurt
- ¼ cup orange marmalade or apricot jam
- 1 teaspoon curry powder
- 1 teaspoon lemon juice
- 1 pound cooked turkey, cut into bite-size pieces
- 2 apples, peeled and finely chopped
- 1 stalk celery, finely chopped
- 1 scallion, finely chopped
- Lettuce leaves (optional)

Equipment

- Measuring cups
- Measuring spoons
- Large bowl
- Spoon for stirring

That looks good, Bert. Let's gobble-gobble it down!

Oh, Ernie!

TIP:
This salad is only very mildly seasoned with curry powder. Add up to 2 teaspoons more to the dressing, if you like it spicy.

"It is I, **Grover**, your world-wide traveler, back from a country called India, where they eat a lot of foods called curry. Curry is a stew that's flavored with many different spices. In America, we make foods with curry powder, which is made from those same spices, mixed together. Smell the spicy-sweet curry powder before you add it to the salad."

grover's Little & Adorable Chicken nuggets

Preparation time: 10 minutes • Baking time: 15 minutes • Makes 4 to 6 servings

Baked with a crispy crust made from crushed saltine crackers, these chicken nuggets received high praise from a panel of kid tasters, who truly seemed to prefer them to the commercial brands.

INGREDIENTS
- 24 saltine crackers
- 1 pound thin-sliced chicken breasts
- ½ teaspoon salt
- 1 tablespoon mayonnaise
- 1 egg white
- 2 teaspoons honey mustard

EQUIPMENT
- Baking sheet
- Large plastic zipper food bag
- Large plate
- Knife
- Measuring spoons
- Large bowl
- Fork for mixing

1 Preheat the oven to 400°F. Lightly grease a large cookie sheet or rimmed baking sheet.

2 kids! Place the crackers in a large plastic zipper bag and zip the bag. Now gently pound on the bag with your fists to crush the crackers into fine crumbs. Pour the crumbs onto a large plate. Set the plate aside.

3 Cut the chicken breasts into 1½-inch squares. Sprinkle evenly with salt.

4 kids! In a large bowl, stir together the mayonnaise, egg white, and honey mustard until well-mixed. Add the chicken to the mayonnaise mixture and gently toss to coat the chicken pieces.

5 kids! Gently press each piece of chicken into the cracker crumbs until the nugget is covered all over. Transfer the nuggets to the greased cookie sheet.

6 Bake the nuggets until the chicken is cooked through, about 15 minutes.

TIP:
To give these nuggets a darker coating, use a whole-wheat variety of saltine-style crackers.

You can dip these in ranch dressing, honey mustard, or plain ketchup. Phew! All this dipping can make a monster a little bit dizzy.

ROSITA'S ham and cheese quesadillas

Preparation time: 10 minutes • Cooking time: About 15 minutes

Makes 4 servings (4 quesadillas)

In Mexico, the country where I was born, people eat a lot of quesadillas.

A true quesadilla (pronounced case-a-dee-yah) is a turnover made from a filled, folded, and deep-fried corn tortilla. In this Americanized version, ham and grated cheese are sandwiched between two tortillas and heated in a dry skillet until crisp.

INGREDIENTS
- 8 flour or other tortillas
- 12 very thin slices deli ham
- 1 cup shredded Cheddar or Swiss cheese
- Tomato salsa (optional)

EQUIPMENT
- Cheese grater
- Medium nonstick skillet
- Wide metal spatula
- Knife

1 Place 4 tortillas on work surface. Top each with 3 overlapping slices of ham.

2 kids! Sprinkle cheese evenly over ham. Top with remaining tortillas.

3 Heat a heavy, medium-size skillet over medium heat. Add 1 quesadilla to the skillet. Cook until bottom is slightly browned and crisp, about 2 minutes. With a wide metal spatula, turn the quesadilla over. Cook until bottom is crisp and cheese is melted, about 1½ to 2 minutes longer. Set aside. Repeat with remaining quesadillas.

4 Allow each quesadilla to cool slightly before cutting into wedges and serving. Serve with salsa for topping or dipping, if you like.

TIP:
The easiest way for parents to cut this quesadilla into wedges is with a pizza wheel or a sharp, serrated knife.

oscar's
favorite fish sticks

Preparation time: 10 minutes • Baking time: 15 minutes

Makes 4 to 6 servings (about 24 fish sticks)

Tartar sauce and yogurt are the "glue" that holds the breadcrumbs onto these baked fish sticks.

> Dip these in ketchup or salsa if you want. What a wonderful grouchy mess!

INGREDIENTS

- ⅓ cup tartar sauce
- ¼ cup low-fat plain yogurt
- ¼ teaspoon salt
- ¾ cup dried breadcrumbs (plain or flavored)
- 1 pound cod fillets

EQUIPMENT

- Baking sheet
- Measuring cups
- Measuring spoons
- Large bowl
- Small bowl
- Large plate
- Knife
- Wide rubber spatula

1 Preheat the oven to 400°F. Lightly grease a baking sheet.

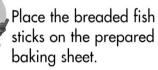

2 **kids!** In a large bowl, stir together the tartar sauce, yogurt, and salt. Spoon half the mixture into a small bowl to use as a dip.

3 **kids!** Spread the breadcrumbs on a large plate.

4 Cut the fish crosswise into ½-inch-wide sticks. Add the fish sticks to the large bowl with the yogurt mixture and stir gently to coat. Dip the fish sticks in the bread-crumbs one at a time and turn them over until they're coated on all sides.

5 **kids!** Place the breaded fish sticks on the prepared baking sheet.

6 Bake the fish sticks until opaque (solid white, not clear) in the center, about 15 minutes. Use a spatula to transfer the fish sticks to individual plates. Serve with a small dollop of yogurt sauce from the small bowl.

Oscar says, "Can you say 'I fixed fresh filleted fish sticks' five times fast? Not bad. . . . Now unscramble your tongue and get lost!"

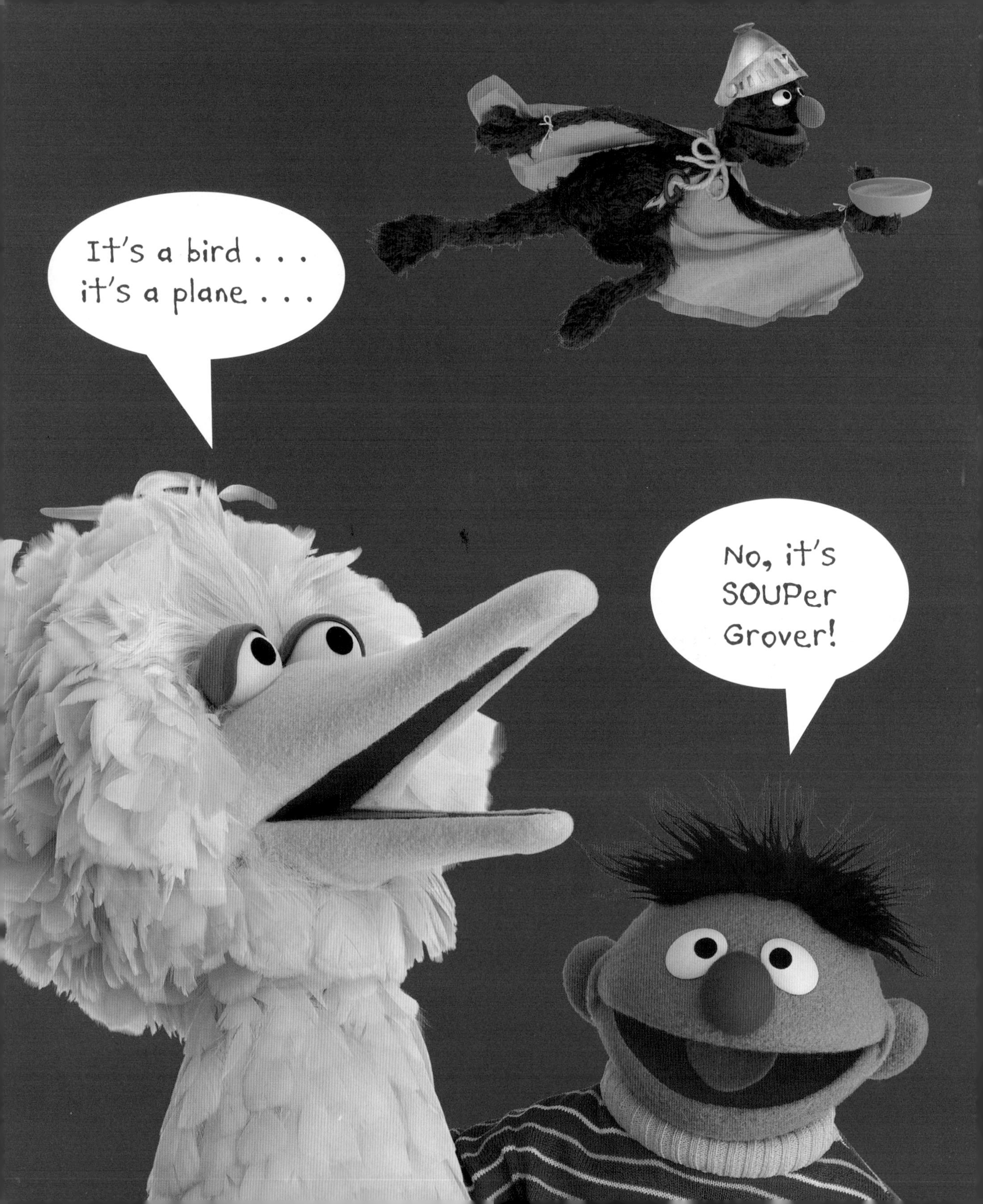
It's a bird . . .
it's a plane . . .
No, it's SOUPer Grover!

SUPER SOUPS

The ultimate comfort food is warm and nourishing and tasty—soup! A small portion of a light soup, such as chicken noodle, is a perfect supper starter. A large bowlful of a hearty soup, such as peanut but-

ter soup or tortilla soup, can be a meal in and of itself—

especially for smaller tummies. And try a refreshing bowl of chilled cucumber soup in the summer; it's so simple and irresistible, your children may say, "Mmm . . . more, please!"

BIG BIRD'S ABC
chicken noodle soup

Preparation time: 15 minutes • Cooking time: 1 hour 15 minutes

Makes 6 servings (about 1¼ cups each)

Cooking the chicken and vegetables in canned broth is an easy and convenient way to add rich, home-style chicken soup flavor.

Sing the ABCs with me as you help make this soup!

INGREDIENTS

- 3 carrots, peeled
- 2 celery stalks, trimmed
- 1 onion
- 1½ pounds chicken drumsticks (about 5 drumsticks)
- 1 can (14½ ounces) chicken broth
- 5 cups water
- 1 bay leaf
- ½ to 1 teaspoon salt (optional; depending on saltiness of chicken broth used)
- ½ teaspoon dried thyme
- 1 cup uncooked alphabet noodles

EQUIPMENT

- Knife
- Large saucepans (2)
- Measuring cups
- Measuring spoons
- Large sieve or colander
- Plastic knife
- Large spoon

1 Cut one of the carrots and one of the celery stalks into large chunks. Cut the onion into quarters.

2 In a large saucepan, combine the cut-up vegetables with the chicken legs, chicken broth, water, bay leaf, salt, if using, and thyme. Heat to a boil over medium-high heat. Reduce heat to low and simmer, uncovered, for 1 hour.

3 Meanwhile, halve and thinly slice the remaining carrots and celery stalk. Set aside.

4 Drain the chicken broth through a large sieve or colander into another large saucepan. Taste and add more salt, if necessary. Add the raw sliced celery and carrot. Heat to a boil over medium-high heat.

5 kids! Fill a 1-cup measuring cup with alphabet noodles.

6 Add the alphabet noodles to the soup. Reduce the heat to medium and boil gently until the noodles and vegetables are tender, about 7 minutes.

Big Bird says, "I found a letter B in my soup. Big Bird starts with the letter B. What's the first letter of *your* name? Try to find that letter in your soup!" What other words start with that letter?

TIP:
You can substitute an equal amount of similarly small shaped pasta, such as tubettini or tiny bows, for the alphabet noodles in this soup.

7 Meanwhile, separate the chicken meat from the bones. Discard the skin and bones along with vegetables from first saucepan.

8 kids! Use a plastic knife to cut up the cooked chicken.

9 Just before serving, stir the cut-up chicken back into the soup. Simmer 1 minute to heat through.

ROSITA'S
TORTILLA SOUP

Preparation time: 15 minutes • Cooking time: 30 minutes • Makes 6 to 8 servings (about 8 cups)

Classic versions of this soup use fried, cut-up tortillas as a topping, but this recipe takes a short cut and uses crushed tortilla chips.

INGREDIENTS
- 1 tablespoon olive oil
- 1 onion, finely chopped
- 2 cloves garlic, finely chopped
- 1 teaspoon chili powder
- 8 ounces turkey breast, cut into bite-size pieces
- 2 cans (14½ ounces each) chicken broth
- 1 can (16 ounces) stewed tomatoes
- 1 can (15 ounces) corn kernels
- 1 ripe avocado
- 2 cup coarsely baked tortilla chips

EQUIPMENT
- Measuring spoons
- Large saucepan
- Can opener
- Wooden spoon
- Plastic knife for cutting
- Measuring cups
- Plastic storage bags
- Ladle
- Soup bowls

1 Heat the oil in a large saucepan over medium heat. Add the onion; sauté until tender, about 5 minutes. Add the garlic and chili powder; sauté 30 seconds. Add the turkey breast; sauté, stirring often, until opaque (white, not clear), about 3 minutes.

2 Stir in the chicken broth and stewed tomatoes with juices, using a wooden spoon to chop the tomatoes into smaller pieces. Heat to boiling over high heat. Reduce heat to low. Stir in the corn. Simmer for 15 minutes.

3 Meanwhile, halve, peel, and seed the avocado.

4 kids! Use a plastic knife to cut the avocado into small cubes.

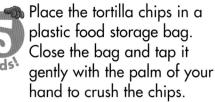

5 kids! Place the tortilla chips in a plastic food storage bag. Close the bag and tap it gently with the palm of your hand to crush the chips.

6 Ladle the soup into individual soup bowls and garnish with avocado and crushed tortilla chips.

TIP: This soup is equally delicious if you substitute cubes of pork loin for the turkey.

Rosita says, "Avocados grow on evergreen trees. Most people think that the avocado is a vegetable, but it's not. It's a fruit!"

oscar's egg DroP SOUP

Preparation time: 5 minutes • Cooking time: 8 minutes • Makes 4 servings (about 4 cups)

Asian foods tend to be high in salt because seasoning ingredients such as soy sauce are high in sodium. This quick and easy recipe calls for low-sodium broth to allow more soy sauce for added flavor.

Dropping eggs is one of my favorite things to do, heh, heh, heh!

INGREDIENTS
- 2 eggs
- 2 cans (14½ ounces each) reduced-sodium chicken broth
- 1 to 2 tablespoons soy sauce
- 1 scallion, trimmed and finely chopped
- 1 clove garlic, finely chopped
- 1 teaspoon dark Asian sesame oil

EQUIPMENT
- Small bowl
- Fork
- Can opener
- Measuring spoons
- Large saucepan
- Wooden spoon for stitrring
- Soup bowls

TIP:
Adding leftover spaghetti or other cooked noodles gives egg drop soup more body and may add to its appeal for some children.

1 kids!
Crack the eggs into a small bowl. (If any pieces of eggshell fall into the bowl, take them out with your fingers before you start stirring. Wash your hands after you've picked out all the pieces of shell.) Then use a fork to stir the eggs well before they're added to the soup.

2 Combine the chicken broth, 1 tablespoon soy sauce, scallion, and garlic in a large saucepan. Heat to boiling over high heat. Reduce heat to low so that the chicken broth is simmering.

3 Gently stir the soup while you add the beaten eggs. Simmer, without stirring, until the eggs are cooked, about 30 seconds.

4 Remove the saucepan from the heat and stir in the sesame oil. Taste and add a few more drops of soy sauce, if you like. Ladle the warm soup into individual soup bowls.

grover's
African-style Peanut Butter Soup

Preparation time: 15 minutes • Cooking time: 20 minutes

Makes 8 side-dish or 4 main-dish servings (8 to 10 cups)

Peanuts supply the protein in this soup, so the chicken and rice are optional. When you add them, however, you have a much heartier soup that can double as a main dish.

This soup is from Africa, where people are just nuts about peanuts!

INGREDIENTS
- 1 cup creamy-style peanut butter
- 1 tablespoon vegetable oil
- 1 onion, finely chopped
- 1 celery stalk, sliced
- 1 sweet red pepper, finely chopped
- 2 cloves garlic, minced
- ½ teaspoon chili powder
- 1 can (14½ ounces) diced tomatoes
- 2 cans (14½ ounces each) chicken or vegetable broth
- 1 cup cooked brown or white rice (optional)
- 1 cup finely chopped cooked chicken (optional)

EQUIPMENT
- Large spoon
- Measuring cups
- Measuring spoons
- Large saucepan
- Plastic knife for cutting
- Wooden spoon for stirring
- Can opener

1 kids! Use a large spoon to stuff the peanut butter into a 1-cup measuring cup.

2 Heat the oil in a large saucepan over medium heat. Add the onion, celery, and red pepper. Sauté, stirring often, until the vegetables are very tender, about 10 minutes. Stir in the garlic and chili powder. Sauté 1 minute longer.

3 Add the tomatoes with their liquid, chicken broth, and peanut butter to the saucepan. Bring to a gentle simmer, stirring often. Stir in the rice and chicken, if using. Cook 5 minutes longer. Serve warm.

TIP: If you're making the soup as a main dish, you can substitute any type of leftover meat in this soup in place of the chicken.

Cute little cukes make cool, cool soup.

grover's
COOL CUCUMBER SOUP

Preparation time: 10 minutes plus 30 minutes chilling time • Makes 4 to 6 servings (about 3½ cups)

Cold soups are great for ready-made lunches and snacks on warm days—make them ahead of time and store them in the fridge. Use the freshest cucumbers you can find for the best flavor; salting the cucumbers before you use them (as directed in the recipe) helps eliminate any bitter flavor.

ingredients

- 3 cucumbers, peeled and halved lengthwise
- 1 teaspoon salt
- 2 small scallions, ends (beards) trimmed, white and green parts separated
- 3 cups low-fat plain yogurt
- 2 tablespoons lemon juice (optional)

equipment

- Metal spoon
- Colander
- Measuring spoons
- Plastic knife for chopping
- Blender
- Measuring cups
- Storage container
- Ladle
- Shallow serving bowls

1 Use a spoon to scoop the seeds out of the cucumber halves. Throw the seeds away. Place the cucumber halves in a colander.

2 Sprinkle the salt evenly over the cucumbers. Place the colander in a sink, and let the salted cucumbers stand for 30 minutes. Drain well.

3 Set aside a small piece of cucumber for garnish, if you like. Coarsely chop the cucumber and the white part of the scallions. Combine the cucumber and white part of scallions in the container of a blender or food processor.

4 kids! Pour the yogurt into the blender on top of the cucumber and onion. Add the lemon juice, if using. Put the cover on the blender.

5 Whirl the soup on medium-high until cucumbers are finely chopped, about 30 seconds, or, if preferred, until completely smooth, about 1 minute. Refrigerate the soup for 2 to 4 hours.

6 To serve, ladle the soup into shallow bowls. If you like, thinly slice the green part of the scallion or the remaining cucumber to use as garnish.

7 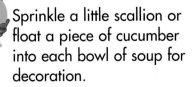 kids! Sprinkle a little scallion or float a piece of cucumber into each bowl of soup for decoration.

Grover says, "Cucumbers and
other green vegetables help your
bones stay strong. Eat lots of green
vegetables and maybe someday you
will be a strong, furry blue monster
like me!"

Brrr! Elmo's Chili!

Preparation time: 10 minutes • Cooking time: 45 minutes • Makes 6 to 8 servings (about 8 cups)

Serve this thick vegetarian soupy-stew with warm corn bread. Like all chilies, this one is even better the next day, after the flavors have had a chance to blend.

ingredients

- 2 large zucchini, halved lengthwise
- 1 tablespoon olive oil
- 1 onion, finely chopped
- 1 sweet green pepper, chopped
- 2 cloves garlic, minced
- 2 teaspoons chili powder
- 1 teaspoon ground cumin
- ¼ teaspoon salt
- 2 cans (14½ ounces each) diced tomatoes with mild green chiles
- 1 can (14½ ounces) vegetable broth or 2 cups vegetable bouillon
- 2 cans (15 ounces each) black beans or kidney beans, or a combination
- 1 tablespoon chopped semisweet or unsweetened chocolate (optional)
- Optional toppings: grated cheese, low-fat plain yogurt, cubes of avocado, finely chopped cilantro

equipment

- Plastic knife for cutting
- Measuring spoons
- Large saucepan
- Can opener
- Wooden spoon
- Ladle
- Soup bowls
- Cheese grater (optional)

1 *kids!* Use a plastic knife to cut the zucchini into thin slices. Set aside.

2 Heat the oil in a large saucepan over medium heat. Add the onion; sauté 5 minutes. Add the green pepper and sauté 5 minutes longer. Add the garlic, chili powder, cumin, and salt and sauté 1 minute longer.

3 Stir in the tomatoes with their juice, vegetable broth, the reserved zucchini, and the beans. Add chocolate, if using. Simmer for 30 minutes, stirring occasionally.

4 Ladle the soup into individual bowls.

5 *kids!* Top each bowl of soup with grated cheddar, plain yogurt, and chopped cilantro, if you like.

TIP:
If your family likes spicier food, try using canned diced tomatoes with jalapeño peppers in place of the tomatoes with milder green chiles.

When **Grover** went to Mexico, the country where Rosita was born, he learned that some people add a secret ingredient to their chili: chocolate! That's right, chocolate! Use 1 tablespoon chopped semisweet or unsweetened chocolate or even some chocolate chips. The chili won't taste like chocolate, but it will have a rich, authentic flavor.

FAMILY DINNER

There are so many benefits to  eating dinners together as a family. It gives you additional family time; it helps your children develop conversation skills; it encourages positive attitudes about food; it has even been linked to higher self-esteem. Your family will come to anticipate mealtime as a special, important part of each day. Now when your children ask "What's for dinner?" you can answer, "What do *you* think we should make for dinner?" They can  choose from this assortment of kid-friendly dishes, among them mini meat loaves, butterfly pasta and flower-shaped carrots, and a pork tenderloin with sweet potato "fries."

Yippee-ai-o!

cowboy elmo's
fastest mac 'n' cheese in the west

Preparation time: 10 minutes • Cooking time: 10 minutes • Makes 6 servings (1 cup each)

This creamy stovetop version of classic macaroni and cheese is just as quick to fix as the boxed variety. Instead of cheese powder, you use American cheese single slices, which instantly melt into a tasty sauce.

Ingredients

- 12 ounces (3 cups) uncooked elbow pasta
- 8 slices American-style cheese singles
- ¼ cup low-fat milk
- 2 teaspoons vegetable oil

equipment

- Large saucepan
- Measuring cups
- Measuring spoons
- Wooden spoon for stirring

1 Heat a large saucepan of lightly salted water to a boil. Add elbow pasta and cook according to package directions until tender, about 7 to 8 minutes. Drain well.

kids!

2 While the pasta elbows are cooking, you can help out by unwrapping the cheese slices. Then tear them up into small pieces so they melt faster when you add them to the pot.

3 Add the milk and the oil to the saucepan. Place over low heat. Return the elbows to the pan along with the cheese. Stir until the cheese melts and a creamy sauce is formed, about 1 minute. Serve at once.

TIPS:
- To reheat leftovers, add a spoonful or two of milk and simmer, stirring often, over low heat.
- If your family likes baked mac 'n' cheese with a crusty topping, transfer the mixture to a 1½-quart baking dish, sprinkle dried bread crumbs over the top, and run under a preheated broiler for a minute or two.

"Yes! I, **Count von Count**, can't wait to find out the number of the day. Here we go . . . 1, 2, 3, 4, 5, 6, 7 . . . 8! The number of the day is 8! Count out 8 slices of cheese for this recipe. As you tear them up to put them on the macaroni, you can count backward, from 8 down to 0."

abby cadabby's enchanting butterflies and flowers

Preparation time: 10 minutes • Cooking time: 20 minutes • Makes 4 servings

It's easy to carve flower-shaped carrots; they'll make this simple, tasty, and pretty pasta dish more fun to eat. You can do it while you're waiting for the pasta water to boil. Bits of chopped parsley sprinkled in at the last minute are the "leaves" that adorn the flowers.

INGREDIENTS

- 8 ounces (2 cups) small egg bow pasta
- 3 carrots, trimmed and peeled
- 1 tablespoon olive oil or butter
- 4 ounces lean ham, slivered
- 1 can (14½ ounces) chicken broth
- ½ cup grated Parmesan cheese
- ¼ cup chopped fresh parsley

EQUIPMENT

- Large saucepans (2)
- Small knife
- Bowl
- Measuring spoons
- Can opener
- Wooden spoon for stirring
- Shallow soup bowls

1 Cook the pasta in a large saucepan of lightly salted boiling water according to package directions until tender, about 8 minutes.

2 Cut each carrot into 2- to 3-inch lengths. With a small sharp knife, carefully carve out narrow, shallow "v" shapes, about ¼ inch apart, around the outside of each piece of carrot. Thinly slice each carrot. (The "v" shape cutouts gives the slices a petal-like appearance.)

3 kids! Put the carrot flowers into a bowl until they're ready to go into the skillet to cook.

4 Heat the oil in a large saucepan over medium heat. Add the carrots and cook, stirring often, until almost tender, about 2 minutes. Add the ham and cook, stirring often, 2 minutes longer.

5 Add the chicken broth. Simmer for 10 minutes. Stir in the Parmesan cheese and simmer, stirring occasionally, 5 minutes longer. Stir in the pasta. Divide among shallow soup bowls.

6 kids! Sprinkle a little parsley into each bowl.

Abby Cadabby asks, "Have you ever seen what happens to pasta when it is cooked? It starts off hard and ends up soft and squishy. It's so . . . enchanting!"

Big Bird's spaghetti pie

Preparation time: 15 minutes plus 10 minutes standing time • Baking time: 25 minutes
Makes 6 servings

Here's a classic use for leftover spaghetti—or a classic reason to make extra spaghetti earlier in the week!

Ingredients

- 2 eggs
- 4 teaspoons olive oil
- ⅓ cup grated Parmesan cheese
- 3½ cups cooked spaghetti
- 1½ cups tomato sauce, such as marinara or meat-flavored
- 1 onion, finely chopped
- 2 cloves garlic, finely chopped
- ½ pound lean ground beef or ground turkey
- 2 carrots, grated
- 1 cup cottage cheese or part-skim ricotta cheese
- 1 cup shredded part-skim mozzarella cheese

Equipment

- Pie plate (9- or 10-inch)
- Small bowl
- Large bowl
- Fork for stirring
- Measuring spoons
- Measuring cups
- Wooden spoon
- Large skillet
- Aluminum foil

1 Preheat the oven to 350°F. Lightly grease a 9- or 10-inch pie plate with vegetable oil or nonstick cooking spray.

2 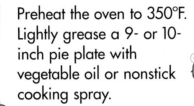 kids! Crack the eggs into a small bowl. (If any pieces of egg-shell fall into the bowl, take them out with your fingers before you start stirring them together. Wash your hands after you've picked out all the pieces of shell.) Then, in a large bowl, use a fork to beat together the eggs, 2 teaspoons of the oil, and Parmesan cheese until smooth. Add the spaghetti and ⅓ cup of the tomato sauce. Toss well to coat.

3 Turn the spaghetti mixture into the greased pie plate.

4 kids! With the back of a wooden spoon, press the spaghetti over the bottom and up the side of the pie plate to form a "crust."

5 Heat the remaining oil in a large skillet over medium heat. Add the onion and sauté until tender, about 5 minutes. Add the garlic and sauté 30 seconds longer. Add the ground meat and cook, breaking up the meat with a wooden spoon, until the meat is no longer pink. Stir in the grated carrot until well-mixed. Turn off the heat and stir in the tomato sauce.

When Big Bird makes spaghetti pie, he invites his pal **Snuffy** over for dinner. Spaghetti is Snuffy's favorite food.

TIP:
Substitute Italian sausage for all or some of the beef or turkey in this recipe, if you like.

6 Spoon the cottage cheese over the bottom of the spaghetti crust. Sprinkle with ½ cup of the mozzarella cheese. Top with the meat sauce mixture. Cover the pie plate with aluminum foil.

7 Bake the pie for 20 minutes. Sprinkle the pie evenly with the remaining ½ cup mozzarella cheese. Bake until the mozzarella cheese melts, about 5 minutes longer. Let the pie stand for 10 minutes before slicing and serving.

cookie monster's me-love-mini-meat-loaves

Preparation time: 10 minutes • Cooking time: 25 minutes

Makes 4 to 6 servings (8 mini meat loaves)

Small meat loaves cooked in muffin cups are done in half the time it takes to bake a regular loaf.

ingredients

- 1 egg
- 1 pound ground meat for meat loaf (a mix of beef, pork, and veal is best for flavor)
- 1 cup uncooked old-fashioned oatmeal
- 1 onion, grated
- 1 carrot, shredded
- ⅓ cup ketchup
- ¼ cup grated Parmesan cheese
- 1 teaspoon salt
- ¼ teaspoon pepper
- Additional ketchup for topping (optional)

equipment

- Muffin pan (12 cups)
- Small bowl
- Measuring cups
- Measuring spoons
- Large bowl
- Wooden spoon for stirring
- Brush (optional)

TIP:
This same recipe works equally well with ground turkey or ground chicken, alone or in combination with other ground meats.

1 Preheat the oven to 350°F. Lightly coat 8 muffin cups with vegetable oil or nonstick cooking spray.

2 kids! Crack the egg into a small bowl. (If any pieces of eggshell fall into the bowl, take them out with your fingers before you start stirring. Wash your hands after you've picked out all the pieces of shell.) Then, in a large bowl, combine the ground meat, oatmeal, onion, carrot, egg, ketchup, Parmesan cheese, salt, and pepper. With clean hands or a wooden spoon, mix until well-blended.

3 Divide the mixture up into 8 equal-sized balls.

4 kids! Place a ball of meat into each muffin cup and press down lightly. If you like, brush the top of each mini loaf with ketchup.

5 Bake until meat loaves are no longer pink in center, 20 to 25 minutes.

eLMo's
Baby Turkey Burgers

Preparation time: 10 minutes • Broiling time: 6 minutes • Makes 8 mini (1½-ounce) burgers

These are regular burgers, made in miniature! For cheeseburgers, a small cube of cheese is buried inside the burger for less mess when broiling.

These burgers taste great with monster—oh, Elmo means Muenster—cheese!

ingredients

- 1 pound lean ground turkey
- 1 tablespoon Worcestershire sauce
- 2 teaspoons olive oil
- ¼ teaspoon salt
- 8 small (½-inch) cubes Cheddar or Muenster cheese (optional)
- 2 to 4 lettuce leaves
- 8 small, soft dinner rolls
- Ketchup
- 8 thin slices plum tomato

equipment

- Measuring spoons
- Large bowl
- Spoon
- Spatula

TIP: You can substitute lean ground sirloin or chicken for the turkey in this recipe, if you like.

1 Preheat the broiler. Adjust the oven rack so the burgers will be 4 inches from the heat source.

2 In a large bowl, stir together the ground meat, Worcestershire sauce, oil, and salt until blended. Divide into 8 equal-size balls.

3 kids! Roll the meat in your hands to make a meatball. Then flatten the meatball between the palms of your hands to make a patty. Place the patties on a broiler tray. If you want to make cheeseburgers, press a cube of cheese into the center of each patty. Check to be sure the cheese cubes are completely buried in the burger patties.

4 Broil the burgers for 3 minutes. Turn and broil until just cooked through, about another 3 minutes.

5 kids! While the burgers are broiling, tear the lettuce leaves into small pieces.

6 Split the rolls and layer ketchup, lettuce, tomato, and burger on the bottom half of each. Cover with the top of the roll and serve.

grover's
chinese meatballs with sesame rice

Preparation time: 20 minutes • Cooking time: 5 minutes for meatballs; 20 minutes for the rice
Makes 4 to 6 servings (about 24 small meatballs)

Once the meatball mixture is ready to shape into balls, start cooking the rice. While the rice is cooking, shape and cook the meatballs. That way, both will be ready to eat at the same time.

ingredients

- 1 pound ground pork or ground turkey
- 6 water chestnuts, minced
- 2 scallions, trimmed and minced
- 2 tablespoons soy sauce
- 1 teaspoon Asian (dark) roasted sesame oil
- 1 tablespoon vegetable oil
- 3 cups hot cooked rice, preferably Basmati, Texmati, or Jasmine
- 2 tablespoons toasted sesame seeds (see Tip)
- 1 scallion, thinly sliced

equipment

- Measuring cups
- Measuring spoons
- Large bowls (2)
- Fork
- Large skillet

1 In a large bowl, combine the ground meat, water chestnuts, scallions, soy sauce, and sesame oil.

2 kids! Use a fork to stir the ground meat mixture until it's well-mixed. Use your hands to shape the meat mixture into tiny meatballs (1- to 1½-inch diameter). Just remember to wash your hands when you're done!

TIP:
To toast sesame seeds, place a small skillet over medium-low heat. Add the sesame seeds and toast, stirring occasionally, until the seeds start to turn golden brown, 1 to 2 minutes. Remove seeds from skillet right away to prevent further browning.

3 Heat the vegetable oil in a large skillet over medium heat. Add the meatballs and cook, stirring often, until browned on all sides, about 1 minute. Cover and cook until meatballs are no longer raw in the center, about 2 minutes longer.

4 Meanwhile, in a large bowl, combine the rice, seame seeds, scallions. Toss well to combine. Serve the meatballs beside or over rice.

Grover traveled all the way to China, where he ate a lot of rice. Grover also learned something he did not know. Instead of growing in fields of soil, rice grows in rice paddies—fields that have been flooded with water. Is that not amazing?

grover's chicken and couscous with juice-juice

Preparation time: 20 minutes plus 20 minutes marinating time • Cooking time: 10 minutes

Makes 4 servings

This sweet dish is sure to be a hit with every family member. Cook the chicken on bamboo skewers (so the pieces cook quickly and evenly all the way around) but take the chicken off the skewers before serving.

ingredients

Chicken
- ½ cup 100% orange juice
- 2 tablespoons honey
- 2 tablespoons soy sauce
- 2 cloves garlic, finely chopped
- 1 pound boneless skinless chicken breast halves, cut into 1½-inch pieces

Couscous
- 1 cup chicken broth
- ½ cup 100% orange juice
- 1 scallion, finely chopped
- 1 tablespoon olive oil
- ½ teaspoon salt
- 1 cup uncooked couscous
- ¼ cup golden or dark seedless raisins

equipment
- Measuring cups
- Measuring spoons
- Large bowl
- Wooden spoon for stirring
- Metal or wood skewers
- Medium saucepan
- Serving platter

1 kids! In a large bowl, combine the orange juice, honey, soy sauce, and garlic. Stir in the chicken until well-mixed. Marinate at room temperature for 20 to 30 minutes or in the refrigerator for up to 2 hours. If using wooden skewers, soak them for 30 minutes before cooking.

2 kids! Prepare the couscous. In a medium saucepan, combine the chicken broth, orange juice, scallion, oil, and salt.

3 Heat the broth mixture to a boil over medium heat. Stir in the couscous and raisins. Cover the pan, remove the pan from the heat and set aside for at least 5 minutes.

When **Grover** traveled to the country of Morocco, he tasted all kinds of foods served with itty bitty pasta called couscous. See if you can find Morocco, in Africa, on a map or globe.

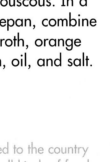

TIP:
If you don't have couscous, serve this dish with similarly seasoned rice. Cook the rice according to package directions, using a combination of chicken broth and orange juice for the liquid. Stir in the scallion and raisins just before serving.

4 Meanwhile, preheat the broiler. Thread the chicken onto 4 large or 8 small skewers. Broil for 2 minutes. Turn skewers, baste with remaining marinade, and broil 2 minutes longer or until chicken is opaque in center.

5 Spoon the couscous onto a serving platter and top with skewered chicken. Remove chicken from skewers before serving.

ernie's Roast Lemon Chicken

Preparation time: 10 minutes • Roasting time: 1 hour 35 minutes plus 10 minutes standing time

Makes about 6 servings

I love lemons. They taste bright and sunny. They look bright yellow and sunny, too— like Rubber Duckie!

Fresh lemon slices and an herb marinade are rubbed under the skin, directly on the meat before roasting. That way, both the skin and the meat have plenty of flavor.

INGREDIENTS
- 1 tablespoon olive oil
- 1 clove garlic, minced
- 1 teaspoon dried sage or thyme
- 1 teaspoon salt
- ¼ teaspoon pepper
- 1 roasting chicken (about 5 pounds)
- 1 lemon, thinly sliced

EQUIPMENT
- Measuring spoons
- Small bowl
- Wooden spoon
- Pastry brush
- Kitchen string
- Roasting pan with rack
- Baster
- Meat thermometer
- Fork

1 Preheat the oven to 400°F.

2 kids! In a small bowl, stir together the oil, garlic, sage, salt, and pepper.

3 Using your fingers, gently separate the skin from the chicken breast, starting at the neck. Brush or rub the herb mixture under the skin, directly on the breast meat. Insert lemon slices between skin and meat. Gently smooth the skin back over the meat. Place any leftover lemon in the neck cavity. Tie the legs with kitchen string. Place the chicken, breast side up, on a rack in a shallow roasting pan.

4 Roast for 20 minutes. Reduce the oven temperature to 350°F. Roast, basting every 20 to 30 minutes, until a meat thermometer inserted in a thick part of a thigh away from the bone registers 180°F and juices run clear when chicken is pierced with a fork, about 1 hour and 15 minutes longer. Remove chicken from oven and let stand for 10 minutes to continue cooking.

TIP:
If time allows, rub the herb mixture on the chicken 30 minutes before roasting to allow the flavors to sink into the meat.

Roast Pork with Bert's Sweet Potato Stripes

Preparation time: 15 minutes • Roasting time: 20 minutes plus 10 minutes standing time

Makes 6 servings

Lean pork is both flavorful and healthful. Paired with sweet potatoes, the roast makes a hearty meal. And to make it fun, you can line up the potato wedges on the plate to resemble Bert's orange striped shirt!

Ingredients
- 1¼ pounds lean pork tenderloin
- 2 tablespoons olive oil
- 2 cloves garlic, minced
- 1 teaspoon dried sage
- 1 teaspoon salt
- 6 medium sweet potatoes, peeled

Equipment
- Rimmed baking sheets (2)
- Measuring spoons
- Small bowl
- Fork for stirring
- Knife
- Large bowl
- Meat thermometer
- Spatula

1 Preheat the oven to 450°F. Place the tenderloin on a rimmed baking sheet or jelly-roll pan. In a small bowl, mix together 1 tablespoon of the oil, the garlic, and sage. Rub the garlic mixture all over the meat. Sprinkle with ½ teaspoon of the salt.

2 Cut each potato lengthwise into 8 spears.

3 kids! In a large bowl, toss the potato spears with the remaining 1 tablespoon oil and remaining ½ teaspoon salt. Arrange the potatoes in a single layer on a baking sheet.

4 Roast the pork alongside the potatoes for 15 minutes or until a meat thermometer inserted into the center of the pork registers 145°F. Remove the pork from oven and let stand for 10 minutes before slicing (the internal temperature of the tenderloin will rise during this standing time). Use a spatula to turn the potatoes over. Reduce the oven temperature to 400°F. Roast the potatoes 5 minutes longer or until tender.

TIP: Ideally, the pork and potatoes will cook alongside each other, but since the size and shape of tenderloins varies (and if you have a thick tenderloin), you may have to leave the meat in the oven for 5 or 10 minutes longer. If necessary, reheat the potatoes in the oven for several minutes just before serving.

"I, **Count von Count**, learned a counting rhyme that's just right for this recipe. You can say it with me:

One potato, two potato,
three potato, four.
Five potato, six potato,
that's all now—no more!"

Something Special on the Side

Vegetables for side dishes come in many shapes, sizes, colors, and flavors. When you go grocery shopping together, point out the bright colors of broccoli or carrots, or the fascinating shapes of squash, or the cute cherry tomatoes. In the kitchen, let your kids see what the vegetables—and fruits, which

often add refreshing flavor to side dishes—look like when peeled or when cut. Then have them help you prepare the salad bar or stack the string beans. It's sure to encourage them to fill their own plates when it's time to eat.

zoe's
Rainbow Salad Boats

Preparation time: 20 minutes • Makes about ½ cup vinaigrette dressing

Set up a small salad bar at home and let everyone choose from an assortment of ingredients. Depending on the toppings chosen, this can be a side dish or a main course.

ingredients

Apple Vinaigrette

- ¼ cup apple juice or cider
- 2 tablespoons apple cider vinegar
- ¼ teaspoon salt
- ⅛ teaspoon pepper
- 6 to 8 tablespoons olive oil

equipment

- Measuring cups
- Measuring spoons
- Small bowls
- Whisk
- Forks and spoons for serving ingredients
- Salad plates

1 In a small bowl, make the salad dressing: Whisk together the apple juice, vinegar, salt, and pepper. Whisk in the oil until blended.

2 kids! Arrange separate bowls of salad ingredients on the table. Give everyone a salad plate and let each person make his or her own salad. Try to "use" as many colors as possible! Use whole lettuce leaves as salad "bowls" or "boats." (Make it safe and easy for very young children to enjoy olives or other foods that are slippery or hard to chew by slicing them into small, thin pieces.) Drizzle a little salad dressing over your salad.

Ooh, how pretty!

TIP:
A salad bar is a good choice for a busy evening. You can choose and prepare most of your ingredients in advance and store them separately in covered bowls in the refrigerator. It's also a great way to introduce your child to new tastes, in small amounts.

- Whole (outer) lettuce leaves to use as bowls or "boats"
- Shredded lettuce
- Grated carrots
- Chopped tomatoes
- Slivered peppers
- Thinly sliced cucumber
- Diced cooked potato
- Diced cooked or grated beets
- Chopped pitted olives
- Cooked green peas
- Cooked chopped green beans
- Cooked chopped broccoli flowerets
- Orange sections
- Apple cut into matchstick pieces
- Sliced starfruit
- Sliced kiwi
- Crushed pineapple
- Diced mango
- Croutons
- Canned beans, such as black, white, kidney, drained and rinsed
- Avocado cubes
- Grated cheese
- Leftover meat in bite-size pieces
- Chopped hard-cooked egg
- Canned tuna

♪ Sunny days . . . ♪

eLMO'S LiTTLe TRees and SunSHine

Preparation time: 15 minutes • Cooking time: 12 minutes • Makes 4 servings

Broccoli and oranges combine to make a "sunny" side dish seasoned with garlic, ginger, and soy sauce.

ingRedients

- 1 head broccoli, cut into bite-size flowerets
- 2 navel oranges, peeled, sectioned, and seeded
- 1 tablespoon vegetable oil
- 1 piece (2 inches long) gingerroot, peeled and cut into ½-inch chunks
- 2 cloves garlic, finely chopped
- ¼ cup water
- 1 tablespoon soy sauce

equipment

- Medium bowls (2)
- Measuring spoons
- Large skillet
- Wooden spoon
- Measuring cup

kids!

1 Put the broccoli "trees" into one bowl and the "sunny" orange sections in another bowl.

2 Heat the oil in a large skillet over medium heat. Add the gingerroot and sauté, stirring often, until golden brown, 2 to 3 minutes.

3 Add the broccoli flowerets and garlic to the skillet. Cook, stirring, until coated with oil. Add the water. Cover the skillet and cook until the broccoli is tender-crisp, about 5 minutes. Remove and discard the pieces of gingerroot.

4 Gently stir in the orange sections and soy sauce. Cover and cook until the orange sections are heated through, about 1 minute. Serve warm.

TIP:
You can substitute 1 grapefruit for the 2 oranges in this recipe.

Abby cadabby's
magic golden zucchini coins

These are so good, they disappear like magic!

Preparation time: 15 minutes • Cooking time: 5 to 8 minutes • Makes 4 to 6 servings

There are two steps to cooking this dish, but it's quick-cooking and sure to become a favorite among squash lovers.

1 kids! Use a plastic knife to slice each zucchini into ¼-inch-thick rounds.

2 In a large saucepan, steam or boil the zucchini until barely tender, 4 to 6 minutes. Drain in a colander and set aside to cool slightly.

3 Preheat the broiler.

4 kids! Place the zucchini in a single layer on a large baking sheet. Sprinkle each "coin" with a tiny pinch of salt and some Parmesan cheese.

5 Broil the zucchini until just golden, 1 to 2 minutes.

ingredients

- 6 small, thin zucchini or yellow summer squash, or a combination
- Salt to taste
- ⅓ cup grated Parmesan cheese

equipment

- Plastic knife for slicing
- Large saucepan or steamer
- Colander
- Baking sheet
- Measuring cups

TIP:
You can steam the zucchini coins, lay them out on a baking sheet, and sprinkle them with cheese in advance, then broil them just before dinner.

BIg BIrd'S sesame green Beans

Preparation time: 10 minutes • Cooking time: 8 minutes • Makes 4 to 6 servings

The peanut sauce in this dish, which is also delicious with carrots, potatoes, and most other vegetables, can be tossed with the beans or used as a dip.

Can you tell me how to make, how to make these sesame beans?

INgreDIenTS

- 1 pound green beans, trimmed
- ⅓ cup smooth natural peanut butter
- 2 teaspoons soy sauce
- ¾ cup water
- 2 tablespoons sesame seeds

equipmenT

- Large saucepan or steamer
- Colander
- Measuring cups
- Measuring spoons
- Small saucepan
- Stirring spoons
- Small skillet
- Large bowl
- Serving bowl (optional)

1 In a large saucepan, steam or boil the green beans until tender crisp, 4 to 6 minutes. Drain.

2 kids! Meanwhile, combine the peanut butter and soy sauce in a small saucepan. Stir in the water.

3 Cook the peanut butter sauce over low heat, stirring often, until thickened and bubbly, about 2 minutes. Cover and set aside.

4 Toast the sesame seeds in a small skillet over low heat, stirring constantly, until the seeds begin to turn golden brown and become fragrant, about 2 minutes. Remove the seeds from the skillet to cool.

5 In a large bowl, toss the green beans with the peanut butter sauce. Just before serving, sprinkle the beans and sauce with sesame seeds. Or put in a bowl and let everyone dip!

TIP:
It's important to remove the sesame seeds from the skillet to cool so they don't continue to cook and burn.

Big Bird's Granny Bird told him that sesame seeds grow in little pods, or seed cases, on flowering plants that can grow very tall. When the seeds are ready to come out of their pod, the pod bursts open with a "pop!" A lot of sesame seeds are grown in the countries of India and China.

Heh, heh, what a great grouchy mess!

Oscar's sticky gooey syrupy squash

Preparation time: 10 minutes • Roasting time: 45 minutes to 1 hour • Makes 6 servings

Roasted acorn squash halves brushed with cranberry-maple glaze make the perfect side dish for poultry or pork. Kids love it because it's sweet and easy to eat.

ingredients

- 3 acorn squash
- 2 tablespoons vegetable oil
- 2 tablespoons butter
- ½ cup maple syrup
- ¼ teaspoon ground nutmeg or cinnamon
- ¼ cup dried cranberries or ⅓ cup fresh cranberries
- Salt and pepper to taste

equipment

- Knife
- Spoons
- Large baking dish
- Measuring spoons
- Measuring cups
- Small saucepan

1 Preheat the oven to 400°F. Halve each squash. Scoop out and discard the seeds and strings. Arrange the squash halves, cut-side down, in a large baking dish. Add enough water to come ¼ inch up the side of the dish.

2 Bake the squash for 30 minutes.

3 kids!

Meanwhile, help an adult put the oil, butter, syrup, nutmeg, and cranberries in a small saucepan.

4 Cook over low heat, stirring often, until the butter melts and the cranberries start to plump up, about 5 minutes. Remove the saucepan from the heat.

Oscar says, "Do you know what a bog is? It's a field flooded with water. And that's where cranberries grow—on vines in cranberry bogs. How terrifically untidy!"

TIP:
You can use dried cranberries or fresh, depending on the season. You can also substitute an equal amount of brown sugar for the maple syrup.

5 Remove the squash from the oven. Turn each half cut-side up. Sprinkle with salt and pepper to taste. Spoon the cranberry mixture evenly into the squash cavities.

6 Bake the squash until very tender, about 15 to 20 minutes longer. Serve warm.

cookie monster's "me-stuffed" potatoes

Preparation time: 15 minutes • Baking time: 1 hour 15 minutes • Makes 4 servings

Leave out the bacon, and these Cheddar cheese-stuffed baked potatoes can double as a vegetarian main dish.

ingredients

- 4 medium Idaho or russet potatoes (about 2 pounds)
- ½ cup low-fat plain yogurt
- 2 tablespoons butter, softened
- 1 tablespoon olive oil
- 1 cup (4 ounces) shredded Cheddar or Monterey Jack cheese
- 3 slices crisp cooked turkey bacon, crumbled
- Salt and pepper to taste

equipment

- Vegetable brush
- Knife
- Measuring cups
- Measuing spoons
- Large bowl
- Large spoons
- Medium baking dish

1 Preheat the oven to 400°F. Scrub potatoes and pierce in one or two places with the tip of a knife.

2 Bake the potatoes directly on the oven rack until tender, about 1 hour.

3 kids! In a large bowl, combine the yogurt, butter, and oil. Stir in ¾ cup of the cheese and the bacon.

4 When cool enough to handle, slice the top off each potato. Carefully scoop out the potato flesh and add to the bowl with the potatoes, leaving a ¼-inch potato shell intact. Place the potato shells in a baking dish.

5 kids! Stir the potatoes and cheese mixture until well-mixed. Use a large spoon to stuff the potato mixture back into the potato shells. Sprinkle evenly with the remaining cheese.

6 Bake the stuffed potatoes in a medium baking dish until heated through, about 15 minutes.

TIP: For a heartier or meaty main-dish stuffed potato, try some of these filling and topping combinations: tuna and olives, chili with toppings, sausage and mozzarella, chicken in cream sauce (chicken à la king), sautéed mushrooms and ham.

Abby says, "Did you know that cheese is made from milk, which comes from cows? Moooo!"

SWEETS & TREATS

The meal was delicious—
so why not finish it off with one last
treat for your sweets? Many of the tasty
dishes in this chapter feature fruit at
their finest, as well as other wholesome
ingredients, such as yogurt or peanut butter. One bite
of any of these desserts will satisfy even the

sweetest tooth. Save the richer selections—
yummy cupcakes with strawberry icing or
the "wow" chocolate cake, for instance—
for extra-special occasions. They're worth
the wait!

eLmo's Beddy-Bye Baked Apples

Preparation time: 5 minutes • Baking time: 12 minutes plus 15 minutes standing time
Makes 4 servings (4 apples)

"Baking" apples in the microwave oven shortens the cooking time by 45 minutes without affecting the flavor. If you use a traditional oven, fill the apples with the cereal mixture before you bake them; cover loosely with foil and bake at 350°F for about 1 hour.

Ingredients

- 4 medium apples (such as McIntosh or Granny Smith)
- ¼ cup muesli, granola, or other flaky or nugget-style cold cereal
- ¼ cup seedless raspberry jam

Equipment

- Peeler
- Knife
- Microwave-safe baking dish
- Measuirng cups
- Small bowl
- Spoons
- Dessert bowls

1 Peel apples two-thirds down from the top. Cut out the core to within ½-inch of the bottom, carving a 1½-inch wide opening at the top.

2 kids! Place the apples in a microwave-safe baking dish, standing up. Add ¼ cup water to the dish.

3 Microwave on High for 12 minutes.

4 kids! Meanwhile, in a small bowl, mix together the cereal and jam.

5 Spoon the cereal mixture into the cored apples. Microwave on High 2 minutes longer or until filling is bubbly and heated through. Remove the dish from the oven and let the apples stand for 10 to 15 minutes.

6 To serve, place apples in individual dessert bowls. Slice or cut into chunks.

TIP:
These apples make a tasty breakfast, too! Use any flavor jam you like or substitute up to an equal amount of honey or maple syrup.

Elmo loves baked apples on cold winter nights. And on warm summer nights. Elmo loves baked apples all the time!

¡Muy deliciosa!

ROSITA'S honey pear CRISP

Preparation time: 10 minutes • Baking time: 25 minutes plus 15 minutes standing time

Makes 8 servings

A little bit of sugar and spice go a long way to turn simple pears into a sweet and delicious dessert.

INGREDIENTS

- ½ cup uncooked old-fashioned oats
- ¼ cup all-purpose flour
- ⅓ cup packed light brown sugar
- ¼ teaspoon cinnamon
- ¼ teaspoon nutmeg
- ⅛ teaspoon salt
- ¼ cup (½ stick) butter, softened
- 4 peeled, ripe Bosc or Anjou pears, halved and cored
- 1 tablespoon lemon juice
- 2 tablespoons honey
- Whipped cream or vanilla ice cream for topping (optional)

EQUIPMENT

- Pie plate (9-inch)
- Measuring cups
- Measuring spoons
- Medium bowl
- Fork for stirring
- Dessert bowls

1 Preheat the oven to 375°F. Coat a 9-inch pie plate with nonstick cooking spray.

2 kids! In a medium bowl, use a fork to stir together the oats, flour, brown sugar, cinnamon, nutmeg, and salt until well-mixed. With your fingers, work in the butter until a crumbly mixture forms. (Don't forget to wash your hands before and after this step!)

3 kids! Place the pears in the pie plate, cut side up.

4 kids! Sprinkle the pears with lemon juice. Drizzle with honey.

5 Crumble the oat topping all over the pears.

6 Bake until pears are softened and topping is crisp and lightly browned, about 25 minutes. Let stand for at least 15 minutes. Spoon into individual dessert bowls. Serve with whipped cream or ice cream, if you like.

Rosita loves the spicy smell of nutmeg. She looked for information about it on the computer and found out that nutmeg is not a nut at all. It is a seed that grows inside the fruit of a nutmeg tree—a kind of evergreen. The seed is ground into powder and used in cooking. ¡Adios!

cookie monster's
peachy dee-licious applesauce

Preparation time: 15 minutes • Cooking time: 15 minutes • Makes 12 servings (6 cups)

How do apples turn into applesauce? Your children will love finding out that applesauce doesn't simply come from a jar.

ingredients

- 10 apples, peeled, cored, and cut into 1-inch chunks (8 cups)
- 2 cups water
- 2 tablespoons lemon juice
- 1 can (15 ounces) peaches in extra-light syrup, drained
- 2 tablespoons packed brown sugar, or more if needed
- 1 teaspoon ground cinnamon

equipment

- Vegetable peeler
- Knife
- Measuring cups
- Measuring spoons
- Can opener
- Medium saucepan
- Spoon
- Plastic kniffe for cutting
- Large bowl
- Potato masher
- Plastic wrap

1 Combine the apples, water, and lemon juice in a medium saucepan. Bring to a boil over medium-high heat. Reduce the heat to medium and simmer, stirring occasionally, until the apples are soft, about 15 minutes.

2 kids! Use a plastic knife to cut the peaches into small pieces.

3 Stir the brown sugar and cinnamon into the saucepan. Simmer for 1 minute. Taste and add more sugar or cinnamon, if you like. Stir in the peaches. Transfer the applesauce to a large bowl. Set aside to cool slightly.

4 kids! Use a potato masher to smash the apples and peaches into a chunky sauce. Cover the bowl with plastic wrap and put the applesauce in the refrigerator so you can serve it cold.

> **TIP:**
> Almost all varieties of apples are good for making applesauce. Some of the best choices include Golden Delicious, Granny Smith, Gala, Jonagold, McIntosh, and Cortland. Try mixing two or more varieties for more interesting flavor.

The Count says, "Today's number is 10! There are 10 apples in this recipe. Count them by 2s. It's easy to skip count: Starting with the number 2, count every other apple: 2, 4, 6, 8, 10 . . . 10 apples all together! Splendid! What wonderful counting!"

ernie's fruity frozen fun pops

Preparation time: 10 minutes • Makes 2 trays ice cube-size pops (32 pops) or 8 to 12 regular-size ice pops

The secret to a successful homemade frozen fruit pop is always to include a banana. That's because bananas freeze well and help give the pop a smooth ice-cream–like texture.

Say fruity frozen fun three times. Fantastic!

INGREDIENTS

- 1 large very ripe banana, peeled
- 1 can (20 ounces) crushed pineapple in juice or 2 cups fresh pineapple cubes
- ¾ cup low-fat plain yogurt
- 2 tablespoons sugar

EQUIPMENT

- Can opener
- Measuring cups
- Measuring spoons
- Food processor or blender
- Rubber spatula
- Spoon
- Ice cube trays (2) or ice pop tray
- Ice pop sticks

1 Combine the banana, pineapple, yogurt, and sugar in a food processor or blender. Whirl on high until very smooth, 1 to 2 minutes, scraping down side of container as necessary. (If you prefer your fruit pops with small chunks of fruit, don't blend quite so long.)

 2 kids! Spoon the banana mixture evenly into ice cube tray cups.

3 Put the ice cube tray in the freezer until partially frozen, 1 to 1½ hours.

 4 kids! Insert a fruit pop stick into the middle of each ice cube tray cup.

5 Return the ice cube tray to the freezer and freeze for at least 4 more hours.

6 To serve, pop the pops out of the ice cube tray just as you would ice cubes.

TIP: Vary the flavor by substituting 2 cups of ripe strawberries or 1½ cups mango cubes for the crushed pineapple.

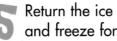

Grover always thought that bananas grow on banana trees. Then he went to South America, where bananas grow, and he found out they don't grow on trees at all. They grow on giant plants that look like trees! Grover is just bananas for bananas!

oscar's QUICK DIP in the mud

Preparation time: 5 minutes • Cooking time: 3 minutes • Makes 4 servings

Fruit is delicious on its own; for a special treat, nothing beats a bowl of melted chocolate for dipping fresh fruit, marshmallows, and cubes of cake.

ingredients

- 6 ounces (1 cup) milk chocolate or semisweet chocolate chips
- 2 tablespoons half-and-half or light cream
- Assorted dippers, such as trimmed, sliced strawberries, banana and apple slices, mini marshmallows, cubes of angel food cake

equipment

- Measuring cups
- Measuring spoons
- Small saucepan
- Stirring spoon
- Dipping cups or small bowl
- Forks for dipping

 1 kids! Combine the chocolate chips and half-and-half in a small saucepan.

2 Cook over medium-low heat, stirring often, until the chocolate is completely melted and the mixture is smooth and heated through, 2 minutes. Divide chocolate dip evenly among four dipping cups (you can use small custard cups, if you like) or for family-style, put into a small bowl. Serve with assorted dippers.

 3 kids! Use a fork to dip pieces of fruit or cake into the chocolate fondue.

Grover says, "Did you know that chocolate is made from cocoa beans? Cocoa beans are found inside pods on cocoa trees, which grow in places with warm, wet climates, such as Nigeria, in Africa, and Brazil, in South America. I went to see for myself, and it was an exciting and tasty adventure. Try to find these places on a map or globe."

TIPS:
- Let the chocolate cool down slightly before serving to young children.
- If the dip gets too thick before it's eaten, pop it in the microwave oven and microwave on High for 10 to 15 seconds at a time, stirring until smooth and melted again.

Looks like mud, but tastes yummy. I mean yucchy! Yucchy! Now scram!

cookie monster's
peanut butter & jelly thumbprint cookies

Preparation time: 10 minutes plus 4 hours chilling time • Baking time: 15 minutes (per batch)

Makes about 5 dozen (60) cookies

These classic cookies are easy for parents to prepare, fun for kids to make, and great-tasting for everyone to enjoy together.

INGREDIENTS
- ½ cup (1 stick) butter, softened
- ½ cup smooth natural peanut butter
- 1¼ cups sugar
- 1 egg
- 2 tablespoons low-fat milk
- ¼ teaspoon salt
- 2 cups all-purpose flour
- ½ cup seedless raspberry jam

EQUIPMENT
- Measuring cups
- Measuring spoons
- Large bowl
- Electric mixer
- Plastic wrap
- Baking sheets
- Teaspoon
- Cooling racks

1 In a large bowl with an electric mixer, beat together the butter and peanut butter at medium-high speed until smooth and creamy. Beat in the sugar until fluffy.

2 With the mixer on low speed, beat in the egg, milk, and salt. Gradually beat in the flour.

3 Wrap the cookie dough in plastic wrap and refrigerate until completely chilled, at least 4 hours or up to 2 days.

4 To bake the cookies: Preheat the oven to 350°F. Lightly grease the baking sheets.

5 kids! Use a teaspoon to scoop the chilled dough into 1-inch balls. Place the balls 2 inches apart on the baking sheets. Flatten the balls slightly, and use your thumb to make a "thumbprint" indentation in the middle of each. Fill each indentation with ¼ to ½ teaspoon of the jam.

6 Bake the cookies until the edges are lightly browned, 12 to 15 minutes. Transfer the baking sheets to racks for 2 minutes. Transfer the cookies from the sheets to the racks to cool completely.

TIP:
You can double-wrap cookies in plastic wrap and freeze for up to one month. Freeze individual portions and use them as little cooler packs in lunch bags. They'll thaw by the time your child is ready to eat and, meanwhile, help keep the rest of the lunch cool.

Why did delicious cookie go see doctor? Dum-de-dum. You give up? Because it felt crummy!

Bert's Best Blueberry Oatmeal Bars

Preparation time: 15 minutes • Baking time: 35 minutes plus cooling time

Makes 2 dozen (24) bar cookies

Fresh blueberries are the surprise ingredient in this classic, easy-to-bake bar cookie.

Ingredients

- 1½ cups all-purpose flour
- 1 teaspoon ground cinnamon
- 1 teaspoon baking soda
- ½ teaspoon salt
- 1 cup packed light brown sugar
- ⅓ cup granulated sugar
- ½ cup (1 stick) butter or margarine, softened
- ½ cup vegetable oil
- 2 eggs
- 1 teaspoon vanilla
- 3 cups uncooked old-fashioned oats
- 1 pint (2 cups) fresh blueberries

Equipment

- 13 x 9–inch baking pan
- Aluminum foil
- Measuring cups
- Measuring spoons
- Small bowl
- Whisk
- Large bowl
- Electric mixer
- Wooden spoon
- Rubber spatula
- Toothpicks
- Cooling rack
- Knife

1 Preheat the oven to 350°F. Line a 13 x 9–inch baking pan with aluminum foil. Lightly grease the foil with nonstick cooking spray or vegetable oil.

 **2 kids!** In a small bowl, whisk together the flour, cinnamon, baking soda, and salt until well-mixed.

3 In a large bowl with an electric mixer at medium speed, beat together the brown sugar, granulated sugar, and butter until fluffy. Beat in the oil, eggs, and vanilla. With a wooden spoon, mix in the flour mixture until blended. Stir in the oats and blueberries.

 4 kids! Use a rubber spatula to spread the batter evenly in the pan.

5 Bake until golden brown and a toothpick inserted in the center comes out clean, 30 to 35 minutes. Transfer the pan to a wire rack to cool completely. Lift by the foil from the pan and cut into 24 bar cookies.

TIP:
If fresh blueberries are unavailable, you can substitute 1 cup of dried blueberries, dried cherries, dried cranberries, raisins, or cut-up mixed dried fruit.

Bert says, "Now what did I want to tell you? Oh, now I remember. I wanted to tell you that eating blueberries (and other blue and purple fruits or vegetables) can help your brain remember things!"

Zoe's Vanilla Cupcakes with Pink Frosting

Preparation time: 20 minutes • Baking time: 15 minutes plus cooling time • Makes 18 cupcakes

The pink color comes naturally to this sweet buttercream frosting because it's made with fresh strawberries.

Ingredients

- 1½ cups all-purpose flour
- 2 teaspoons baking powder
- 1 teaspoon baking soda
- ¼ teaspoon salt
- ½ cup (1 stick) butter, softened
- 1 cup sugar
- 2 eggs
- 1 cup (8 ounces) low-fat plain yogurt
- ½ teaspoon vanilla

Strawberry Buttercream Frosting
- ½ cup (1 stick) butter, softened
- 4 strawberries, hulled and cut up
- 2½ cups confectioner's sugar
- ¼ cup half-and-half
- 1 teaspoon vanilla

Equipment

- Muffin pans (for 18 cupcakes)
- Cupcake liners
- Measuring cups
- Measuring spoons
- Medium bowls (2)
- Spoons for mixing
- Large bowl
- Electric mixer
- Plastic knife
- Toothpicks
- Cooling rack

1 Preheat the oven to 350°F. Line 18 muffin cups with cupcake liners. Set aside.

2 kids! In a medium bowl, stir together the flour, baking powder, baking soda, and salt until well-mixed.

3 In a large bowl with an electric mixer on medium-high speed, cream together the butter and sugar until light and fluffy. Beat in the eggs, one at a time. With the mixer on low speed, beat in the flour mixture alternately with the yogurt, beginning and ending with the flour mixture. Beat in the vanilla. Pour the batter evenly into the lined muffin cups.

4 Bake the cupcakes until golden on top and a toothpick inserted in the center of each comes out clean, about 15 minutes. Transfer the pan to a rack to cool completely.

5 Meanwhile, prepare the frosting: In a medium bowl with an electric mixer on high speed, cream the butter until it is pale and fluffy. Add the strawberries; beat for 30 seconds. With the mixer on low speed, add the confectioner's sugar, ½ cup at a time, until well-blended. Add the cream by spoonfuls, beating until blended. Add the vanilla and beat until fully incorporated.

6 kids! Spread the frosting evenly over the cool cupcakes with a plastic knife.

Hey, that looks like my tutu. And it tastes too-too yummy!

ELMO'S hooray, it's my Birthday! chocolate cake

Preparation time: 20 minutes • Baking time: 25 minutes plus cooling time • Makes one 8-inch layer cake (8 servings)

This is a quick, one-bowl special-occasion cake that gives children lots of stirring to do! It's made with yogurt and applesauce but still has plenty of rich flavor to satisfy the chocoholics in your house.

ingredients

Cakes
- 2 eggs
- 1¼ cups sugar
- 1 cup (8 ounces) low-fat plain yogurt
- ½ cup applesauce
- ⅓ cup vegetable oil
- 1 teaspoon vanilla
- 1½ cups all-purpose flour
- ½ cup unsweetened cocoa powder
- 1¼ teaspoons baking soda

Frosting
- ½ cup (1 stick) butter
- 2 ounces (⅓ cup) milk chocolate chips or milk chocolate candy bar, chopped
- ⅓ cup unsweetened cocoa powder
- 2 teaspoons vanilla
- 2 cups confectioner's sugar
- 2 tablespoons low-fat plain yogurt

1 Preheat the oven to 350°F. Lightly grease and flour two 8-inch round cake pans.

2 kids! Crack the eggs into a small bowl. (If any pieces of egg-shell fall into the bowl, take them out with your fingers before you start stirring them together. Wash your hands after you've picked out all the pieces of shell.) Then, in a large bowl, stir together the sugar, yogurt, applesauce, oil, eggs, and vanilla until smooth. Sift in the flour, cocoa powder, and baking soda. Stir until smooth and well-blended.

3 Divide the batter evenly between the two prepared pans.

4 Bake the cakes until a toothpick inserted into the centers comes out clean, about 25 minutes. Cool cakes in pans on racks for 10 minutes. Turn cakes out onto racks to cool completely.

5 kids! Meanwhile, prepare frosting. Combine the butter and chocolate bar in a small saucepan.

6 Melt butter and chocolate over low heat, stirring until smooth and blended. Pour into a large bowl. Stir in the cocoa powder and vanilla.

TIP:
A quick, kid-pleasing way to decorate a cake is to simply cover it in rainbow sprinkles.

EQUIPMENT

- Cake pans (two 8-inch)
- Small bowl
- Measuirng cups
- Measuring spoons
- Large bowls (2)
- Wooden spoon
- Sifter
- Toothpicks
- Cooling racks (2)
- Small saucepan
- Cake plate
- Spatula

7 kids! Stir in 1 cup of confectioner's sugar and the yogurt. Stir in the remaining sugar until the frosting is smooth and spreadable.

8 To frost the cake, place one layer on a cake plate. Cover with a layer of icing. Place the remaining layer on top of the first. Spread the remaining frosting with a spatula over the top and sides.

Elmo says, "Elmo's birthday is February 3. When is your birthday? Try to find it on a calendar."

SnACKS

Children's tummies are small, so kids often get hungry between meals. A nutritious snack can give them a needed boost of energy and help them make it to the next meal. Here are some quick, fun, and yummy snack ideas. Most will be favorite and familiar foods to your child; other tastes may be new. Keep in mind that children may not accept a food until it's been given to them ten or so times. Don't give up!

What is Ernie's favorite snack?

Cheese and Quackers!

Sesame Street Sesame Sticks
Wrap thin slices of turkey around bite-size sesame-coated bread sticks or thin pretzel logs.

Big Bird's Squishy Eggs
Halve hard-cooked eggs. Mash the yolk with a little plain yogurt and mustard. Stir in finely chopped pimiento-stuffed green olives. Fill the hollow in the egg white with the yolk mixture. Press the two halves back together before serving.

Grover's Superhero Salad Rolls
Layer thinly sliced meat and spreadable cheese on soft lettuce leaves. Roll the leaves up tightly from one long end.

Rosita's Hot-Hot-Hot Bagel Pizzas
Preheat the broiler. Slice mini sesame bagels in half and spread with salsa. Sprinkle with grated Cheddar or Jack cheese. Place on a foil-lined pan and run under the broiler for a minute or two until the cheese melts.

Zoe's Cool Pink Strawberry Soup

For each serving, combine 1 cup 100% orange juice, 3 or 4 trimmed strawberries, and a spoonful of sugar, if needed, in the container of a blender. Whirl on high until you have a thin puree. (Fruit that isn't quite ripe enough will require a spoonful of sugar.) Pour into a shallow bowl and serve with a swirl of plain or vanilla low-fat yogurt.

Cowboy Elmo's Veggies and Ranch Dip

The quickest way to do this is to serve an assortment of precut veggies and bottled ranch salad dressing (or other creamy dressing) for dipping. A healthier way is to stir together 1 cup low-fat plain yogurt, ¼ cup whipped cream cheese, ¼ cup mayonnaise, 1 finely chopped clove of garlic, and a little salt. This dip has essentially the same flavor as ranch dressing but the yogurt makes it healthier and you can control the amount of salt. You might even try making it without the cream cheese and mayo. The garlic and salt may add just enough flavors to satisfy young taste buds.

Abby Cadabby's Make-It-Yourself Rainbow Fruit Kabobs

Set out bowls of fresh bite-size fruit chunks and let your child assemble her own rainbow kabob by skewering the fruit onto ice pop sticks. Serve with lemon (or other fruit-flavored) low-fat yogurt as a dipping sauce.

Ernie's Frozen Bananas

Peel firm-ripe bananas. Place on baking sheet and freeze for 1 hour. Wrap each semi-frozen banana individually in aluminum foil; double wrap in plastic wrap. Freeze at least overnight. Partially unwrap to serve. (It will taste just like banana ice cream!)

Remember the time we went apple picking?
How sweet it is!
And then Elmo made yummy applesauce!

Together Time

Cooking together isn't the only way to have fun at mealtimes. Here are some more ideas:

1. Make a "theme" meal. Design your own or try these:
   - Pick a color: a meal at which all the foods are one or two colors, such as yellow and green for a sunny spring day.
   - Pick a shape: a meal at which all the foods are round, for example, from meatballs to peas to blueberries.
   - Pick a letter: a meal at which all the foods start with the same letter.

2. Encourage your children to help decorate the table:
   - Purchase a plain white paper tablecloth. Spread it out for your kids to color with crayons or markers.
   - Have them create a centerpiece with some small stuffed animals, or colored marbles in a jar, or anything else they dream up.
   - Think of some fun new ways to fold up napkins. Choose some colorful napkin varieties to dress up the table.

3. Try table talk:

   As much as possible, sit down for meals together and encourage everyone to join the conversation.
   - Go around the table and have each person pick a favorite food from the meal (or any favorite food) and describe why he or she likes it. Try to use a variety of terms, such as "sweet," "crunchy," "juicy," and so on, to help build your children's vocabulary.
   - Talk about family events, such as picnics, reunions, or holidays and what the special dishes are for that occasion.
   - Talk about places you have gone together, encouraging children to talk about what you saw, whom you visited, and what you ate—perhaps it is going to Grandma's house for homemade peach pie and ice cream or apple picking in the fall.
   - Share some jokes. Here's one to start: "Why did the fruit salad look so lonely? Because the banana split." Adults may groan and roll their eyes, but wordplay is lots of fun for kids.

Funny FOOD Faces

Grover, Ernie, and Bert look good enough to eat! See if you can find all the little foods at the top of the page in the big pictures.

Try making your own funny food faces at home!

raisins

tomato

blueberries

Food sculpture by Laurent Linn. Photographs by John E. Barrett.

olives   lemon   pasta   radish

licorice   orange

About the Authors

Susan McQuillan is a nutritionist and food writer who has written extensively about

healthy eating. She has contributed many articles and recipes to magazines such as *Woman's Day, Family Circle, American Health, Prevention,* and *Cooking Light.* Susan has a lot in common with Cookie Monster; she loves to eat healthy foods like fruits and vegetables, but she also loves cookies! Susan would like to thank Elmo and the rest of the Sesame Street gang for teaching her daughter Molly all about the ABCs and 1-2-3s, and for all the bright ideas they inspired for this cookbook.

Leslie Kimmelman has worked at Sesame Workshop for many years. She is the

author of more than two dozen books for children. She divides much of her spare time between reading in the living room and cooking in the kitchen.

Elmo is tickled—er—red to be working on a cookbook. "Elmo loves good food," says the little red guy. "Elmo wants to know what foods *you* like."

Big Bird prefers birdseed milkshakes, birdseed sandwiches, and birdseed salads. But he's always open to trying new foods. "I've tried every recipe in this book—and they're all delicious," he promises.

Cookie Monster says, "Me liked writing and cooking recipes in book—but me LOVED eating them!" Cookie thinks all food is dee-licious, but guess what he likes best!

Rosita is crazy about mangos, avocados, and other fruits and vegetables that remind her of Mexico, the country where she was born. Rosita wants to say *gracias* to Susan McQuillan. "Thanks for letting me help with the cookbook."

Grover is a world traveler, a part-time taxi driver, and a waiter. However, it's this cute, furry blue monster's first stint as a cookbook writer. Some of his favorite things to eat? A tasty and healthy (super) hero sandwich, of course, or some of the little and adorable chicken nuggets he helped prepare for this book.

Ernie is known for his love of a good joke and his love of a good bath, with Rubber Duckie, of course. He also loves to cook, especially with bananas. His favorite snack is cheese and quackers!

Bert is fond of bottle caps, paper clips, playing the tuba—and oatmeal. He would like to thank his favorite pigeon, Bernice, for inspiring his work on this cookbook.

Zoe tried many new foods while working on this book, such as zucchini, which begins with the same letter as her name does. Zoe knows that eating healthy foods gives her energy to dance.

Oscar the Grouch refused to provide any information about himself. "Go away!" he grumbled. It's rumored that his favorite foods are rotten apples, sardine sundaes, and mud pies.

Count von Count is often too busy counting food to actually eat it. Did you know there are more than 50 recipes in this book and 128 pages? Count your favorites!

Abby Cadabby is the newest neighbor on Sesame Street. She comes from a long line of fairies and loves the magic of learning to cook. And don't worry if you spill any milk. Spilled milk is fairy food!

Index

Italicized page references indicate photographs.

Did you count the twiddlebugs like this ? There are 58.

Thanks for cooking with Elmo! Elmo would love to meet in the kitchen again sometime soon!